"Educators will immediately connect with The F
stories that will prompt you to reflect, encourage y
inspire you to dream! With a focus on relationsh.   ..p you
to build your own personal strength and thrive fr... the collective strength
of others. Take a journey with this EduGladiator and get ready to take on the
future of education."

—Jacie Maslyk, Assistant Superintendent, speaker, author of
*Connect to Lead, STEAM Makers: Fostering Creativity and Innovation in
the Elementary Classroom*, and *Remaking Literacy: Innovative Instructional
Strategies for Maker Learning, Grades K–5*

"Rachelle Dene Poth reminds us through the power of storytelling that our
history, voice, and values mold us into the people we are for our students.
Continuing to grow, learn, and evolve as professionals pushes us to be more for
our students than we knew we could be. Poth expertly weaves the foundation
of being an educator with how to engage in new learning adventures while
supporting students, so the reader best understands how we can both celebrate
our strengths and individuality alongside teamwork, collaboration, and
learning."

—Mandy Froehlich, speaker, consultant, author of
Divergent EDU and *The Fire Within*

"Rachelle's book, *The Future is Now*, inspires educators to create chaos in
classrooms, to break with traditions, and to be committed to finding new
ways to make better and longer-lasting change for our students. This book
asks the tough questions, provides motivational quotes, and serves as a road
map for being the change agent your students and teachers need you to be.
With a deft hand, Rachelle guides us to find our power, to build the strength
of others, and know how to gladiate together by sharing her journey and
those of other educators."

—Laura Steinbrink, instructional technology coach and
HS English teacher, @SteinbrinkLaura

"Rachelle's book had me at 'The Future.' Whenever I read her work, Rachelle always seems to take another step toward amazingness. The thing that works best in this book is that she skillfully connects important themes in education, gathers stories from educators, and then puts it into practicality for her audience. We've got skill, relational work, breaking traditions, and my favorite, disrupting. We can't move forward with light speed if we don't look back. Pick this book up, even if you aren't an educator and prepare to move forward exponentially."

—Jeff Kubiak, educator, author of *One Drop of Kindness*, speaker and #Kidsfirst advocate for #AllKids

THE FUTURE
IS NOW

Looking Back To Move Ahead

RACHELLE DENE POTH

EduGladiators

Image Credits:
Carlie Antsis
Brent Clarkson
Manuel Herrera
Shelby Krevokuch
Amber McCormick
Dana Ladenburger
Heather Lippert
Scott Nunes
Chris Spalton
Tisha Richmond
Monica Spillman
Laura Steinbrink
Wanda Terral
Kitty Tripp
Julie Woodard

Paperback ISBN: 978-1-7336864-4-0
E-book ISBN: 978-1-7336864-5-7

Published by EduGladiators LLC
www.edugladiators.com

Book Design & Production: Columbus Publishing Lab
www.ColumbusPublishingLab.com

Printed in the United States of America
1 3 5 7 9 10 8 6 4 2

I've learned that it is not what I have in my life, but **who** I have in my life that counts.

—Anonymous

Mom and Dad, thank you for being the best parents a person could ask for. You've always been there to support me through all of my adventures in life, learning and growing. Because of your belief in me, I learned to believe in myself.

David, thank you for listening and encouraging when I needed it the most, and for always taking care of things so that I could do the work that I am passionate about.

A lot of people have gone further than they thought they could because someone else thought they could.

—Anonymous

Many thanks to "My 53s" for being the best friends a person could hope to have in their life. To the #4OCFPLN, thank you for joining me on this journey.

Thank you to my EduGladiators family. I am honored to be connected with you and thankful for the friendships that we have formed. Thank you for believing in us and for your inspirational leadership, Marlena Gross-Taylor.

CONTENTS

PART III: GATHERING STRENGTH AND GLADIATING TOGETHER

OUR STORIES

Throughout this book you will hear from educators with different backgrounds and different roles in education. My hope is that sharing their stories will inspire you to share yours. Through our stories we can encourage, uplift, and inspire action to prepare our students and ourselves for the future. Are you ready for the challenge? The future is here, waiting.

FOREWORD

Dennis Griffin Jr.

One of the most exceptional qualities our children possess is the innocence that is accompanied by their ability to dream. The dreams of a child are often filled with passion, adventure, positive self-images, and the vision of success. The dreams of a child are often connected with an accomplishment of grandeur that exceeds the dreamer's highest expectation. Other times, the dream materializes from the example someone else has set. Through their dreams, children can visualize the change they desire to be in the world. The dreams of a child are not distorted by race, gender, socioeconomic status, or creed. The ability of children to dream is limitless. The power of their dreams can be the spark to inform the direction of their lives. And then . . .

Our children stop being dreamers.

I am not sure when or how this happens, but at some point our social circles, school systems, and media outlets rob our children of their ability to dream. The dreams are replaced with the labels that our systems have predetermined for them. The systems reinforce the labels through feedback that creates fear and doubt. The fear and doubt that is created becomes powerful enough to dictate the outcomes of our children's lives by diminishing the power of their ability to believe in themselves. Believing in yourself, your purpose, and your values can create a vacuum of isolation that is difficult to withstand for adults, let alone children. The system provides us with two choices: chase your dreams or accept a label and fit in. However, when you are an EduGladiator, you have only one choice: follow your dreams and protect the dreams of others. Adhering to the normalized structures of the status quo ostracizes dreamers. Harriet Tubman was a dreamer. She dreamed of freedom. Tubman's dream called her to action to not only free herself but to free her brothers and sisters who were victims of slavery. Her dreams aligned with her purpose, a purpose that was greater than herself. This purpose was evident in her nineteen different freedom liberations on the Underground Railroad that freed over three hundred slaves.

Today, the thought of slavery is admonished, and Harriet Tubman is a heroine who defied a system of oppression. However, during the 1800s, her dream was ridiculed and could have cost her her life. Dreamers' ideas are often challenged and deemed unsuccessful if they fail. The Wright brothers were dreamers who believed they had the power to fly. They were unsuccessful; they were ridiculed and mocked. However, the Wright brothers used their strength, patience, and passion in order to revolutionize our ability to travel around the world. They persevered in the pursuit of their dream. Many of our students have received and accepted the messages of a hidden curriculum that essentially communicates that it is better to accept the label the world will give you than to make your dreams become a reality. The thought of being challenged and potentially failing has denied an unlimited number of dreams from becoming a reality. If you do not believe me, think about the limits that you have placed upon yourself or that others have tried to place upon you. Did you have a dream that you stopped pursuing because of feedback, doubt, fear, criticism, or isolation? What was your dream when you answered your calling to serve as an educator? What steps are you taking to make that dream become a reality? Did something happen that stopped you from following your dream? How can we get you back on the path to following your dreams? How can we make sure that our children are not detoured on their journey?

James Allen, author of *As a Man Thinketh*, stated, "Humanity cannot forget its dreamers; it cannot let their ideals fade and die; it lives in them; it knows them as the realities which it shall one day see and know."

I became an educator because I wanted to reach for the stars to change the world. In my mind, reaching for the stars is not just a symbolic representation of achieving my dream. I interpret the stars in Harriet Tubman's quote as our children and the bright potential they possess in the shroud of the dark sky. During Tubman's time, the stars (especially the North Star) guided her to freedom. Today, the North Star is education. The ability to obtain a high-quality education is one of the pillars that creates the freedom to pursue our dreams. The dreams of our children have the power to light the path for future generations. My dream now is to be an agent of change who creates an educational system that empowers students to aspire to use their gifts and talents to accomplish their dreams. Think about it: when we pursue our dreams, we achieve a level of freedom that is often hard to capture with words. The problem is that without the proper supports, our children's stars fade, their light begins to extinguish, and they become lost in the darkness. The change our world needs will happen only when we reach and impact the lives of all children. We often forget that inside of us is the strength, patience, and passion for challenging the status quo.

Strength

It takes strength to accept your calling. We need strength to fight self-doubt, labels, and criticism that impede our ability to protect the dreams of our students. The strength that is needed must be taught to our students. It takes strength to dispel the inaccurate perceptions of students, classrooms, and schools that often create generalizations that validate the status quo. Our students need to understand that failure and setbacks are part of the learning process. The only way they will learn this is if educators model the process of learning from failure. It takes strength to take ownership of your students' outcomes beyond when they are in your classrooms, embedding a seed of excellence that manifests years down the road. It takes strength to be the model the students look to for strength.

When I run into my former students, many of them are excited to see me again. Honestly, I think I am more excited to see them. I make sure to ask them what they are currently doing in their lives. For some of them, there is a brief moment of despair that I see on their countenance and in their eyes, as my former students express that they are not where they thought they would be in life at this moment. I take a moment to ask them, "What are your dreams?" I always tell them they are exactly where they are supposed to be on their journey. I then ask them one of the most important questions I could ever ask: "What are you willing to sacrifice to accomplish your dreams?" I ask them what their plan is to achieve their goals. I tell them that, in order to accomplish their goals, they are going to have to overcome their fears, and they will need the strength to know that they might lose friends on the journey. I make sure to tell them that to achieve a dream is not an easy task and it takes the strength of mind, character, and spirit to make their dreams a reality. I let them know that I believe they will bring their dreams to reality because I saw the potential within them when they were my students. I share that I, too, encountered many setbacks, but I never gave up. I remind them that Mr. Griffin's students never give up. I believe my goal of being a change agent is to breathe life into the dreams of others. As a matter of fact, let me tell you that you are exactly where you are supposed to be on your journey. Harriet Tubman had strength and so do you. The real test of your strength happens over time.

Patience

Educators crave immediate gratification so much that we have underestimated the power of patience. We are human. Instant gratification provides a sense of accomplishment that has the potential to impact how we view ourselves. We are often worried about how our students will perform and who will judge us. We worry despite knowing that everyone learns differently, and the pace of learning is also different for everyone. We worry despite understanding that we learn from mistakes and second chances.

When I entered the classroom, my mindset was to be the change in education. The change in education that I envisioned was not just about the current academic progress of my students. I wanted to make sure that my students had the opportunity to pursue their dreams, goals, and ambitions. I wanted to make sure my students knew that they had a support system. I knew that, although my vision would take years to manifest, it would become a reality as long as I planted and nurtured the seeds inside my students. I can tell you in the world of education the most significant rewards that I have ever experienced occur when my students reconnect with me—when they tell me that they have gone to college, have a job, are starting their career, or have started a family, and they share with me that I made a difference in their lives. I cannot describe the gratification that I feel when they tell me they hope that their children will have a teacher like me one day. This gratification means more to me than any score on a standardized assessment or any plaque. Without patience I would have never been able to experience what true gratification is.

Passion

The eyes serve as a clear indicator of the burning passion that is within someone's heart. Your passion will have you asking how you will use your gifts to impact others instead of asking how your gifts will allow you to profit in this world. Passion provides the ability to question the status quo and create new ways of looking at the world and new opportunities in spite of the criticism, ridicule, doubt, fear, and isolation that may confront you on your journey. The burning desire to confront the status quo to provide excellence for all children is your passion. There is a chance that you will fail; however, passion says failure is a better option than maintaining the status quo. Our passion allows us to say that every experience is a learning experience that gets us one step closer to our destination. My students are my passion. My commitment to my students ensures that I plant a seed of belief within them by creating a learning environment that engages all students in the learning process that will transform their lives. Their dreams are mine to protect. Passion ignites your courage and becomes contagious to those in your sphere of influence. My passion enlarges my courage, as I am determined to make a difference in the lives of my students. Passion is the torch that must be passed on to future generations as they continue to be the light that inspires the next generation of dreamers.

The Stars

Harriet Tubman's dream of creating a world where all men and women would be free was filled with strength, patience, and passion. Her passion did not bring her any financial gain. Her passion opened the road to think about what was possible. Dreams must be protected because they are the torch that must be passed on to future generations as they continue to be the light on the journey of change. The dreamers are the stars in the night sky that provide hope for a better tomorrow. What freedom will your dreams unlock in our students?

CHALLENGE

Take a few minutes to write down how you protected the light of a star in your class. Share your story with the hashtag **#FUTURE4EDU.**

References
Allen, J. (1924). As a man thinketh. Girard, Kan: Haldeman-Julius Co.

Dennis Griffin Jr. serves as the principal of Brown Deer Elementary School in Brown Deer, Wisconsin. He has seven years of experience as a middle school educator and is entering his fifth year as an administrator. He is currently pursuing his doctoral studies in educational leadership at Cardinal Stritch University. Dennis believes all students will be successful in school when they develop relationships with educators who value their gifts, cultures, and individuality.

Introduction

THE FUTURE IS NOW:
LEARNING AND GROWING TOGETHER

I often wonder to myself, *Where does the time go?* You wake up one day and it hits you. Years have passed by; life has changed so much, and it doesn't show signs of slowing down. Our days have become so hectic and filled. So many responsibilities to attend to, challenges to face, decisions to be made—and some days can be tough. Those are the days when I miss my childhood. Even at my current age, when I come across old pictures, hear a certain song on the radio, find a childhood knick-knack, or have a random thought that sparks a childhood memory, it takes me right back to being a kid. But I am not a kid anymore.

Growing up, there were times when I thought that being a kid wasn't so much fun and I couldn't wait to be older. As a teacher, I often hear students say they can't wait to graduate, to be out on their own, and it reminds me of times when I felt that same way. As a child, I had moments when I wanted to run away. I even packed a few things in a bag, but I wasn't ever serious; it was just a frustrated kid's response. All it took was a teacher's phone call home and my desire to avoid being grounded and I wanted to escape. As a teenager, there were times when I couldn't wait to be out on my own. Graduate high school and head off to college and be independent. Except when I finally was, there were days that I wanted to be back at home. And even though I'm happy where I am in life, and work on improving each day, sometimes I do feel a little sad.

Sad for missed opportunities along the way, time that could have been spent with family, making moments count, or thinking about what I would do differently if given the chance. At some point throughout the day, every day, I catch myself wondering what might have been, asking myself a lot of what-if, could-I-have, should-I-have questions, wishing for another chance to make a different decision. Another opportunity to go in a different direction with my life. These thoughts or times when we question ourselves and our decisions can consume us if we let them. But before that happens, reality kicks in and we know that going back is not possible. I'm sure every single one of us would go back and change at least one thing or do one thing a bit differently if we could. But then again, would that one thing change the trajectory of our lives so much that we wouldn't be where we are today? It might.

It's easy to sit back and wonder what might have been, but we can't really change anything. The "I wonder ifs" will only cause us to feel bad. We make our choices based on the knowledge we have at the time, or sometimes on impulse. Either way, we often don't get a second chance. So the best that we can do is to live fully in the present and prepare for the future by drawing upon our past. Reflect. Whatever past experiences you wish you could redo, use them to plan forward starting today. Make a different choice now, with the knowledge you have. The future is now. We are living it and we don't have any way to slow it down. Time will pass by and we can lose ourselves in the chaos that our days might bring. The closest we can come to slowing down is if we stop our momentum, but it won't do us, or those we lead, any good in the long run. We are all works in progress and need to keep evolving, because the future is now.

In the Blink of an Eye

No matter how much you wish it didn't, life keeps coming at you. Sometimes it comes at you pretty hard. Maybe that's why I think about my childhood often. I felt much safer then and didn't have so much to worry about. I was an only child with very supportive parents and grandparents from whom I learned the importance of family, hard work, trying new things, and being kind to others. Looking back, I was an odd child with strange interests and went off the beaten path sometimes. I was definitely *different*.

Have you ever looked at old pictures and almost felt embarrassed by the kid you were? When you see yourself dressed in some bizarre outfit, or doing something you thought was funny at the time, but now you wonder what you were thinking? Or maybe that was just me. How many kids out there got excited to have office supplies and play school? (I was the teacher and the student.) Or had parties with their stuffed animals as the guests? And of course, I had a few cats that joined in these activities too, which probably surprises no one. These were just a few of my favorite after-school activities. I made the best of being an only child. (I even have the pictures to show it!)

Keeping childhood memories fresh helps me to be mindful of what it is like growing up, hoping to fit in, and trying to figure out who you are. When I look at my pictures or my childhood treasures packed away in the boxes at my parents' house, the memories come flooding back. There are times when I laugh or roll my eyes at myself, and other times when tears fill my eyes because certain memories resurface. Have you ever had days when it just hits you, and you realize your age and wonder how that happened? Where did the time go and why did things have to change so much? Yet, when you pick up something from your childhood or you think back to a fond memory, it feels like it was not quite so long ago. It can feel strange. Think about your own life experiences, explore your memories, and compare who you were when growing up with the person you are today. Were there any signs throughout your childhood of who you might become?

Time Capsules: Looking Back To Predict the Future
What Did School Teach You?

How often do you look back at your childhood memories? Personally, it's like going on a treasure hunt. I'm always fascinated by the kinds of things that my parents kept and, of course, the things that I managed to keep over the years. (Not sure why I kept so many folded notes.) My mom tries to get me to store the boxes in my own house, but for some reason I think that if I do, I will lose track of exactly where each item is, and then my memory will start to fade. My "time stamp" will be lost forever. Knowing where these things are enables me to travel back in time, if only briefly. There are some interesting things in those boxes: *Goonies* and *E. T.* trading cards, Hello Kitty everything, cassette "mix tapes," notes that my friends wrote (all folded up, of course), an Oscar the Grouch alarm clock, records, stuffed animals, concert tickets, and lots of random childhood souvenirs. I can remember specific times in my life so clearly just by seeing these. My school memories take up the space in most of the boxes. There are projects, notebooks, old worksheets, drawings, and report cards. As a teacher, I find it interesting to look back at my work to figure out the kind of student that I was. I know what the report cards said, but I like to see teacher comments on my assignments and projects. So much red pen covering my work, some critical comments, and a few stickers here and there. It's interesting to compare those practices to my own practice as a teacher.

Looking at them, sometimes I try to see if there were any signs of what my future might hold. If you have a box of memories, a photo album, or even videos of your childhood, take some time to explore and see if you can make any "predictions" about your life now based on your childhood. Or use the items to think about what kind of kid you were. It is interesting to take time to reminisce. I look at the pictures I drew, or read entries in my diary, to see if I had any big dreams back then. But I can't say that I've ever found anything that reflected something about my life now with any accuracy, until my mom found a letter that I had written to my parents, dated back in 1985.

Making a Deal

Apparently I understood more about contracts than I was aware of in law school. The letter to my parents was actually called a contract, and was the first contract that I wrote. The purpose? I wanted to be able to hang out at the mall with my cousin. Back then, hanging out at the mall all day, spending time in the record store, was my favorite thing to do, so I wrote a contract. The "letter," written in cursive and in a rather formal, legal manner, set out my demands and also added in the "consideration," in contract language, of what I would do in return. My promises included cleaning without being asked, studying, doing my homework, not asking to go to the mall, and getting straight As on my tests. I included a place for my parents to sign and date it, but apparently they never agreed to the terms, as they did not sign it. I've looked at it several times since my mom gave it to me, and I find it interesting that it somewhat relates to my life today, being an attorney as well as a teacher. But I still wonder: Who was I as a child? Where did I learn to write an agreement like that? And why didn't my parents sign it? Seriously. That is something that I need to find out. It's funny that a contract written at the age of thirteen was better written than a contract I created in law school twenty-five years later!

Belonging and Fitting In

I was an interesting kid, definitely a bit different then and now. I remember feeling like I didn't fit in, no matter how hard I tried. And maybe that was the problem. I wanted to be friends with who I thought were the "cool kids." Was I trying too hard to be somebody else? Was I trying to be just like them? I think I was, but I wasn't like them. Being a kid can be tough. So instead, I spent time with a few friends, my parents, or my grandparents, and I was more than okay with that. My favorite times were going to the mall or a drive-in movie with my parents, helping my grandma set up her bingo cards, hanging out with my grandpap for Friday night bowling, and sleepovers at my grandparents' houses. I appreciated the simple things. I don't remember asking my parents for a lot—not too much anyway—but there were some things that I really wanted when I was a kid. And they weren't the traditional games or toys that other kids wanted, maybe because I didn't have siblings to play the games with. I was happy with things like big coloring books, train sets, and games I could play by myself. I was a huge fan of games involving strategy, especially computer games, and I loved getting books, Barbie dolls, and stuffed animals. There's a perception that if you're an only child, you have everything you want. I guess for some that might be true, but it was not true for me. I had everything that I *needed*, but what I wanted most was to fit in and be around people. I always wanted more time with my parents and grandparents. But a bigger part of me really wanted to feel "normal" and accepted. I kind of wanted to be someone else.

If I Could Be Anyone . . .

Back in the late 1970s, when I wasn't in school, I spent my time playing on the computer, watching TV, or listening to my latest record while singing quietly and dancing in my room. If you had asked me who I wanted to be, I would have named two people. (Apparently my inability to make a single decision was evident then just as it is today.) I absolutely loved Olivia Newton-

John, and I remember playing *Grease* as a kid and fighting with my friends and cousins over who would get to play the role of Sandy. Thinking back now, though, I'm not really sure how you "play" *Grease*, but playing *Grease* meant that we recited the lines and sang along with the soundtrack to act out the movie. I've often wondered how many other kids did the same thing, or if it was just another one of my odd quirks. Definitely a quirk.

My parents took me to see Olivia in concert when I was in the seventh grade. Talk about a dream come true. I remember like it was yesterday. The concert was at the Civic Arena in Pittsburgh; they opened the roof for the concert, and I'm pretty sure that's when Olivia was singing "Xanadu." Pure magical moment. I was also pretty good at roller skating, and when I saw the movie *Xanadu* I was absolutely mesmerized. (In the movie, Olivia skates and sings). Seeing her in concert was a magical and surreal experience for me. I was fascinated by Olivia Newton-John and I wanted to be just like her.

Forms of Power

Besides my dreams of being Olivia, I also really wanted to be like Wonder Woman. I have so many memories of spinning around in my driveway, and I'm sure my neighbors thought that I was a strange child after that, if they didn't already. I believed everything that I saw on TV, and my hope was to transform into Wonder Woman right there in my driveway. My mom had some gold cuffs, and sometimes I would put them on, thinking I would transform into Wonder Woman. I watched the show so much as a kid. I was fascinated by this woman with a cool job and awesome superpowers. She could change in an instant and go to help others who were in need. Wonder Woman just knew. Somehow she was able to sense that somebody out there needed help. Without hesitation, she dropped what she was doing, spun into costume, and went to the rescue. So what was it about Wonder Woman that intrigued me?

Maybe it was the costume, maybe it was those gold cuffs, maybe it was just the idea of being a superhero. Regardless of what my fascination was with Olivia Newton-John and Wonder Woman, I think that, as a child, the lesson I learned was that women had the power to do amazing things. I think I've always had that inner desire to be Wonder Woman, wanting to help others, to have superpowers that could help others in need.

A few years ago, when I saw the modern *Wonder Woman* movie, I felt all sorts of nostalgia. For me to actually go and see a movie, it had to have been something awesome, as I don't often see movies anymore. I was totally drawn in by the storyline. Maybe partially due to my childhood dreams, I was captivated by the story and the memories I had of spinning around, hoping to transform into Wonder Woman. I may have even spun around in the parking lot after the movie.

Determination

For me, Wonder Woman represented a strong, courageous woman who was not afraid to step away from what she had always known and venture out into places she didn't know existed. She left her home and everything she knew without looking back. She was not afraid of the challenges that rose up before her. Even though people tried to make her stay behind or get her to back down from the direction she was heading, she persisted and fought through it all. She knew that she had to help others. Even in what seemed to be a moment of defeat, she gathered her strength and emerged victorious. Even in situations where she was wounded or had been knocked down, she got right back up to continue fighting and pursuing her passion: helping others and fighting for good. She was fearless and strong and believed in herself. She bravely took risks so that she could do what was right for others. She believed that this was her true purpose.

Humility

Wonder Woman was always mysterious, ready to go to the rescue of those who needed her, whenever and wherever they were. She was humble and had a sense of humor, sarcasm, curiosity, and wit. She didn't ask for thanks, nobody knew who she really was, and to everyone connected with her she was just Diana Prince. But even in her real identity, she had all of the same characteristics of Wonder Woman. She was thoughtful, intuitive, resilient, and tenacious. For me, and I'm sure other fans, even though she was a fictional character, Wonder Woman served as an inspiration for many young girls and women. I think that might hold true as much now as it did back then. Wonder Woman was a role model for me as a child, and even as an adult now, I can understand why people admire superheroes and their powers. Why do we identify with or aspire to be superheroes? Maybe because superheroes are seen as fearless, humble, curious, compassionate risk takers who persevere and inspire others to act.

Courage: Educators and Superheroes

Educators are superheroes, and I believe that students are superheroes as well. We may not always see it, but there are times when our colleagues or the students in our classrooms step up and do something for the good of someone else, and they don't wear a fancy costume or possess anything mysterious about them. They just know when to step in, help others, and do everything they can to make sure that their "work" is done, and then they just go right back to what they were doing. They don't stand around waiting for thanks, they don't ask for recognition, and they don't want any type of reward. Mostly they are very humble beings who put others before themselves and are genuinely invested in making the world a better place. Sound familiar?

Rarely do superheroes share all of their stories, but they should. Sharing stories can provide others with the courage they need to use their own powers, or sharing can offer the hope that others may need to continue on. We don't always know the stories of our colleagues or our students, and sometimes we don't even truly know ourselves. Moments happen when we are pushed against a wall, or something happens that propels us to take an action. We find power and strength that we didn't even know we had.

Think about the power of superheroes. Do they know from the beginning that they have special powers, or do they discover them, and then struggle with how to use them, and how to act? I think it is a mix. But if I'm keeping with Wonder Woman, she had a mentor who believed in her and pushed her to not settle for anything less than being her best. The mentor kept her grounded but encouraged her to push through failures and struggles, to become a better version of herself every day. Isn't this what we are supposed to be doing for our students? Think about students you have worked with, or maybe even someone who has worked with you, who helped you to push through challenges and inspired you to not give up. What would it be like if you did not have that experience? What would it mean for the person you are now?

Finding Your Power: The Power Within

It can be scary to put yourself out there, but educators do it every day, and I'm guessing that sometimes this carries over into our real life as well. What I mean by "real life" is life after we leave the classroom. There is this power or innate trait that educators possess, which enables us to recognize a weakness or a need in others, whether our students, friends, families, or colleagues. We have the power to help others find their way. It's by instinct that we take care of others and rise up to help when we are needed. Some of us are born with these powers and others continue to develop them over time, perhaps because they were traits in a person that we wished we had.

Maybe you don't think of yourself as a superhero, but you should. It's not about being someone who is larger than life and better than everyone else. Educators don't need to wear capes or have any special props, and there doesn't have to be anything unique about our appearance. It's about using our talents to do what's right and what's best for others. As educators, we have the tremendous power to make an impact and influence the lives of the students we teach and learn from every day. We get to start fresh every single day and have new chances to use our powers and refine our skills so that we can be the best versions of ourselves for our students. How many other professions can say the same thing? We have the opportunity to bring about changes that will make an impact on the lives of not just one student but many students, and our colleagues as well.

For some superheroes, it may take some time to realize the superpowers exist. It might be later on in life that you realize you have a certain strength or skill. Or maybe you have a weakness that has been an area of struggle for your whole life, and somehow, either something or someone has enabled you to turn that weakness into a source of strength, a strength you use to help others. We all have mentors, whether or not they are clearly identified or defined. And sometimes it's because of our mentors that we realize that we have a superpower; we just needed some guidance to know how we can use it for the good of others.

> I think a hero is an ordinary individual who finds strength to persevere and endure in spite of overwhelming obstacles.
> —Christopher Reeve

My Superheroes

We have all had superheroes, and I've had several superheroes through-out my life: people whom I have looked up to and admired because of who they are and their impact on others. When I was a kid, and up to this day, my parents have been my superheroes. My mom has always supported me and pushed me to try things way outside of my comfort zone. Many times she had more confidence in me than I did in myself. I learned not to give up too easily. I remember different times in my life when I was really struggling with things and I wanted to quit. My mom persisted, telling me that I could do whatever it was, so I kept on going until I did. She has always given good advice, even if as a teenager (and sometimes as an adult) I did not always want to hear it. I've often heard the phrase "a mother always knows." Although I haven't always wanted to believe it, my mom was usually right about most things. As an adult, I admire her because she continues to challenge herself, push outside of her comfort zone, and it inspires me to do the same.

Growing up, I was always amazed by my dad. Anyone who knows him would probably say the same thing: he is the nicest guy who would do any-thing to help you. There are so many times that my dad has offered his help to others without hesitation or concern for how much time it might take. There have been many times that I have doubted myself, worried about making the wrong decision, afraid to take a chance on something, and my dad has always been there to offer advice, to help me think something through, or to empa-thize with me if something did not go well. He is compassionate and a great mentor who inspires me to be better each day.

I am fortunate to have such supportive parents, my first teachers and superheroes, because they helped me to develop what I refer to as my "in-ternal compass." This compass, formed from the guidance of my parents, helps me to navigate through difficult decisions and challenges. It is an inner voice that guides me in the right direction. My parents have always been there to see me through and believe in me; I count on them for advice almost every day.

Besides my parents, my grandparents were my superheroes too. They had this tremendous strength to make me feel better when I was sick, to brighten my days when I was feeling sad, to teach me lessons of life that you can't learn in school. They were always giving of themselves and putting others' needs before their own. Superheroes. Humble, resilient, compassionate, and driven.

Life will always have challenges and uncertainties. Regardless of what they are, remember that you can push through them by being surrounded with family and friends and a powerful PLN (personal or professional learning network). Keep moving forward, dare to be different, to dream big, and to be a source of strength for others.

You are a superhero even if you don't think so. You have a special trait or unique, authentic quality about you that makes you distinct from everyone else. Everyone is a superhero in some way because there is somebody somewhere looking up to each one of us. And we might not even realize it, but our students, our families, our peers are often looking to us as a source of guidance or strength. Remember that you have the power within to dream big, to do more, and to achieve great things. It won't always come easily, but it will be worth it.

Anyone can give up; it is the easiest thing in the world to do.
But to hold it together when everyone would expect you to
fall apart, now that is true strength.

—Chris Bradford

Part I

BUILDING OUR STRENGTH

The essential conditions of everything you do
must be choice, love, passion.
—Nadia Boulanger, French Composer

Chapter 1

EVERYBODY HAS A STORY: WHAT IS YOUR *WHY?*

What Makes You *You*

So what are your superpowers? You have them, even if you can't state exactly what they are. You possess a skill, a characteristic or something unique about you that leads others to count on you. Think about your strengths and weaknesses. When people think about you, what are some of the things that come to their mind first? This is a hard question that I've been asked and struggled with answering myself. Questions like these are some that I have even asked my students throughout the year as part of our ongoing relationship-building. I have also asked them, "What are some interesting characteristics about you? What do you consider to be your best traits or skills? What is something that I might be surprised to know about you?" I have also asked some simpler questions about favorite foods, types of pets, or bands. I really wanted to hear from them about what they believed about themselves. I wanted to learn more about them and their "special powers" and interests. My goal was to help them discover what unique skills and traits they possessed but may not yet have realized, and to find things they had in common with their peers.

Have you ever tried something like this? If so, how did it go? Getting answers from my students was not too easy. Some students thought it just wasn't "cool" to talk about themselves. Several responded with general information that they had skills in sports, enjoyed writing poetry, loved drawing, and so forth. A few confidently shared personal experiences such as struggles with an illness or even a learning disability. Hearing these stories actually helped the other students become more comfortable with sharing something about themselves, and it gave me a better understanding of who my students were. For whatever reason, some students felt that talking about their strengths would be perceived as bragging or trying to "outdo" their classmates. For the first time, I heard some students refer to a peer as a "try-hard," which, according to them, is a person who volunteers in class or asks questions. Apparently participating in class—being a "try-hard"—is a bad thing. I'm not sure where these ideas come from, but when I heard these comments, it created a teachable moment for them as much as me. Together we talked about why it is important to ask questions, to share our stories, and to connect with one another in class. We need to understand what makes us unique and how we can use our talents to help others.

The Power of Storytelling

Sharing our stories and experiences brings great power. When we share our strengths as well as our weaknesses, we let people in and open ourselves to a system of support that we can rely on in a time of need. People need to know what you are passionate about, what you can do well, your strengths and motivations. But they also need to know your struggles and how you have overcome them even when you felt you could not (and maybe even wanted to give up). People need to know that you have experienced failures and how you got yourself back up and moving forward again. This is where the story begins. It is time to share yours. Be vulnerable and inspire others to do the same.

Think of educators you know who seem to have everything under control. And then think of those educators who look like they need help with organization, classroom management, or improving their practice. Are you basing your decisions on conversations that you've had with them, on observations, or on your own perceptions? Until we make those connections and share our stories, we don't really know what our colleagues or our students are experiencing. That's what makes these conversations so important. Without them, we determine or negotiate our understanding of people and situations based only on brief observations or possibly even what we hear from others. Without these stories, we won't know that others are struggling too. This is why we must always share our truths, or others will create them for us.

There is power in sharing stories. We truly need to share our ups and downs, because if we don't, then we are limiting our opportunities for support and professional growth. And if we are struggling, then how will we succeed without that support in place? And more importantly, how will we help our students to succeed? We need to be able to identify our own signs of strength and weakness and those same signs in others. We will then know when we need to seek help for ourselves and when to step in to help others.

Thinking about Your *Why*

How many times have you been asked, "What do you do for a living?" This seems to be a common question when you first meet someone, or when you are in a group of people and those awkward moments of silence happen (and you've already talked about the weather, latest news, or other current trends). Showing an interest in others and asking questions are natural parts of the conversation. I've been asked this question many times—easy enough to answer. But on many occasions, I've been thrown off by the question that often follows: "Why?" In the awkward silence as I struggled for a response, I found that I didn't know. Even students have pushed my thinking by asking why I am still teaching or why I would want to be a teacher instead of working as an attorney.

When people have pushed on finding out my *why*, usually my answer was that teaching was my job and I enjoyed it, but I did not have an inspirational story to share. My initial thought (and what I almost said) was that it was my job, my income. Instead, my typical answer was because I enjoyed foreign languages. That's it. It was the best answer that I could think of at the time. There wasn't any mention of having a love of teaching. Unlike other educators I knew, teaching was not a lifelong dream that began when I was a child. Playing school as a kid was fun, but becoming a teacher was not something that I ever thought about doing as an adult. What made me stay in the profession if it was "just a job" to me? How had I gotten into this profession in the first place? Because I would never have predicted it for myself many years ago. Even now, twenty-five years after college graduation, there are days I wonder how I got to be where I am today. And sometimes I even ask myself why I'm still here. Not often, but some days are tough to get through; frustrations happen and I question whether I am where I am supposed to be. Do you ever feel the same way? Think about why you got into teaching. Was it a choice that you made, a second career, or did it just sort of happen? What has made you stay in the profession?

Lessons from Childhood that Led Me to Teaching

Looking back to my childhood, I recognize some signs that point to why I might have ended up in education. I had an aunt who taught French and several uncles who were teachers and guidance counselors. My grandpap Berquist (my dad's father) loved teaching me how to speak French. I even taught myself some Spanish while waiting at my cousin's house for a ride to school every day. And I also really enjoyed playing school. For Christmas one year I even received a student desk. There are pictures that exist as evidence that at some point in my life, I actually enjoyed sitting still in those student desks.

As an only child, I did not have any friends around to play with most days when I got home from school. My grandma or grandpap would be waiting for me and stay with me until six thirty when my parents came home from work. A few nights I didn't even see my dad, as he was attending night school to obtain another degree and studying for the CPA exam in addition to working full-time. Seeing my dad continue to seek additional degrees while working full-time definitely inspired me to be a lifelong learner.

So most days after school it was just me, no siblings, and none of my school friends lived close by. To pass the time, my grandma would quiz me on the state capitals or times tables, encourage me to practice the piano after my lessons, or have me help her with some cooking (I was great at making pudding). But on many days, all that I really wanted to do was play school. We had this bookcase with a pull-down desk that I thought was the coolest thing ever. It became part of my "classroom." As both teacher and student, I passed time creating, completing and grading my own assignments. I had different "classrooms" set up in my house, and at one point I even used the dresser in my room, a cardboard box, and some office supplies for my teacher desk.

It got lonely playing both roles, so sometimes my stuffed animals were my students, lined up in a circle in the basement. I loved the idea of being the teacher, even if I was the student, too, or my stuffed animals had to be. It was fun for me and I didn't notice being alone as much.

Learning about Teaching

Starting in sixth grade, I became involved in working with my teachers. My favorite elementary school memory was staying after school to decorate the bulletin boards or hang student work in the hall with Sister Bartholomew. She was tough, especially when it came to discipline, but I had a connection with her, and helping her in the classroom gave me a purpose. In 1983, when I was in the seventh grade, my school received a few Apple computers, and I stayed after school with Mr. Anders at least twice per week to learn how to program. Other days I would go home to teach myself how to write my own programs, excited to show my parents what I had created. A few of us were

INNOVATION HASN'T avoided St. Agnes School. Here instructor Walter Anders works on a

so interested in the cool computers that the local newspaper came to our school to do a story, which led to my first time being photographed for a newspaper: two students and their teacher, seated in front of two gigantic Apple computers, looking completely mesmerized. The wording under the picture read "Innovation." I still have that newspaper clipping, and whenever I look at that photo it absolutely amazes me when I compare the world of today with the world back then.

Aside from the changes in how people look when it comes to clothing, and definitely the hairstyles, it is a picture that could have been taken in a classroom today: teachers and students working and learning together, powerful learning made possible when there is access to the right resources that enable us to enhance and extend learning. With an image like this, you cannot even tell who is doing the "teaching" and who is doing the "learning." Everyone is a learner. Who could have predicted the changes from then until now in how, when, and where we can learn. I was brave and shared that picture with my eighth-grade STEAM classes. Aside from some laughter, and a few students asking which one was me, they became really curious. They mostly asked questions about the computers, if I ever made predictions of what the future might look like, or if I imagined things like cell phones, virtual reality experiences, and artificial intelligence when I was their age. Not really. There were TV shows and movies that depicted life in the future, but it was not something that I put a lot of thought into. At that point in time, I thought that the tech was already pretty amazing.

It is so interesting to compare our school experiences and look at the

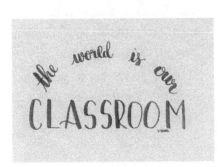

digital transformation and its impact on education over the past thirty-four years since I was in the eighth grade. Being able to show old types of tech and see student reactions is awesome, and it reminds me how much I love teaching now and having those moments to connect with students.

When I talk with them about the changes and how learning is different now, I always have the same thoughts:

- We no longer have to be in the same physical space to learn together.
- We are not limited to learning that happens from the teacher or the other students in the classroom.
- Computers and technology enable us to flatten the classroom walls and communicate globally.
- The world becomes our classroom. I wonder what changes these students will see in their lifetime.

A Teacher's Assistant

Never had I thought about going into education, even though I had been in classrooms for many years of my life and spent time as a child in my aunt Val's classroom while she taught. It made me happy to help pass out papers and grade tests. I enjoyed the "teaching" opportunities with my aunt, and those other times when I played school as a child. But I never thought about being a teacher, and I don't recall even considering any professions except briefly during my senior year of high school when I developed an interest in becoming an optometrist. I can't remember what even gave me the idea of thinking about that as a career. I remember doing a little research on it, but it was only a passing thought and not one that I seriously considered.

In high school I did well in most of my classes, but at some point between my junior and senior year I lost some of my ambition, and started to feel the pressure of heading off to college. I wasn't afraid of going to college, but I was nervous about making a decision about my future and what I wanted to study. When the time came, I chose "undecided" as a liberal arts major. At least it was a start.

Decisions Are Hard

After several meetings with counselors during my sophomore and early junior years at Penn State, I still had not decided on what I wanted to do. We started to eliminate possibilities based on courses that I had or had not taken, or grades in courses that I did take. A lot of effort was spent trying to sort through my skills and my interests. During my junior year, a major in education was one of the last options suggested. I never thought about becoming a teacher until I had to make a decision so that I could graduate. I would not graduate in the traditional four years, and I hoped to need only one additional semester of study. After a few phone conversations and one or two more meetings, I decided to declare secondary education as my major. When I say I decided, I don't even believe that it was truly a decision that I came up with on my own.

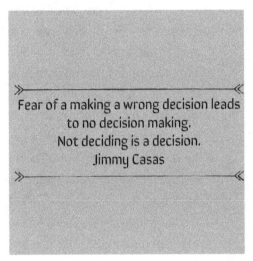

Fear of a making a wrong decision leads to no decision making.
Not deciding is a decision.
Jimmy Casas

Part of me hesitates in making a lot of decisions, as though the need to decide will disappear. Declaring a major is a big decision to make, and I have always struggled as a decision maker. If I need to choose one option, I choose two. If it's two, I want three. I always find a way around it, rationalizing and apologizing for my indecisiveness. It's a struggle with doubting myself and that persistent fear of making the wrong decision. For a few years I enjoyed the comfort of still being an undecided undergraduate. I loved learning and probably would have chosen to be a student forever if I could. We know, realistically, that is not an option. But the status of being undecided was a security blanket that I was clinging to so tightly. And it was time for me to get rid of that comfort, because I was running out of time.

Preparing for Life through Mentoring

This is a huge decision that young adults must make and one that I am happy to not have to make again. I often see my students struggling to decide what to study after they graduate, where they want to go to college, or even if they want to go to college at all. They often worry that they aren't good enough, that their grades won't be high enough to get into their first-choice school, basing their "value" on a grade point average. Everything comes down to an average and trying to meet some standard, a way to measure ourselves against others. Maybe that's why I feel that I can relate to them—because I've been there and I've had those same struggles. I can listen to their concerns and, to an extent, share my own experiences, but I cannot decide for them. This is something that I wish someone would have or could have done for me. The best I can do is listen, support, and offer encouragement, but I don't want to influence their decisions at all. I simply want to be someone whom they can turn to and who supports them without judgment. This is what I needed, and had, as I struggled with my own decisions back then and even now as an adult.

YOU MUST DO THE THINGS YOU THINK YOU CANNOT DO.

– ELEANOR ROOSEVELT

@Manuel_herrerati

Amy Storer, Instructional Coach,
Keenan Elementary School, Montgomery ISD, @techamys
Over five years ago, my campus principal, Sonja Lopez, asked if I would be interested in taking on an additional role on our campus. The role was called Campus Academic Technology Support, and we were commonly referred to as CATS. At the time, I had little to no experience with technology integration or support, and I could have never predicted where one small word would take me.

"Yes."

That was all it took to change the course of my educational career. I often think back to that phone call and wonder what would have happened if I didn't "do a thing that I thought I couldn't do." She took a risk on me so I could take a risk for myself. Every risk and chance that I have taken has led me to exactly where I am meant to be. Those risks are a part of my foundation, and although scary at times, they were totally worth it in the end.

I am now an instructional coach at Keenan Elementary School and the lead technology integration mentor (TIMS) for my district. Those small and sometimes large steps led me here, but my journey isn't over. Is it ever really?

•••

Learning To Trust Yourself

There were times during my undergraduate education when I was afraid I would not make it through. I had a terrible GPA my first semester, which definitely shook my confidence, and I think for the first time I realized that I was on my own. I also felt like a failure; it was not like anything I had experienced before. People can be there to help you, but nobody can do it for you. You can work around things, but in the end, you can't take shortcuts and expect that it's going to be enough. I was thankful that I had the kind of upbringing I did when it came to school and learning. My parents had prepared me well and taught me the skills that I needed—I just had to figure out how to apply them on my own. I had to trust myself to make my own decisions and know that, even if I made the wrong decision, I would be okay and I could figure it out.

In life there will be struggles and failures. This is something that we all experience but don't always share. Maybe it's a fear of feeling inadequate, embarrassed, like more is expected of us—so how can we let others know that we aren't there yet? We need to share more often. What makes the dif-

ference in dealing with failure is how you work through it. We can't let our struggles or failures define us. Many times that is exactly what I did, feeling as though I was not meeting a standard, that the expectations held for me were higher than I could reach. I often felt ashamed that I had not done well, or that I was letting people down. It felt like failure happened to me often. Such feelings can break our confidence and limit our potential for growth. We have to act upon our failures and find the value of learning within them to help us become better each day. When we do this, we can use these experiences to help others who might be going through the same thing. We won't ever know unless we start first by sharing our experiences and being vulnerable.

Find Your Voice So Students Can Find Theirs

My education came first. My parents spent time studying with me, working with me to understand what I was learning, and helping me to find the resources I needed. They connected with my teachers, which was not always a high point for me. Apparently I was quite social in the classroom and would often speak out during class. In elementary school, frequent calls were made to my parents because, no matter how many times the teachers would change my seat, I would still talk. I would make friends wherever I was in the classroom, and it apparently interfered with the teaching and learning back then. I think this kind of holds true for me today. I will say I don't like public speaking, but according to some of my students, whenever I have been given a microphone, I won't stop talking. I have to admit that they might be right—to an extent. Many times I have shied away from speaking, especially in public or in front of my own colleagues. I've often doubted myself, thinking that I would not have anything valuable to add. However, during the past five years, when it comes to talking about education and my students' work, I want to share our stories. My passion for education, for doing what is best for my students, led me to find my voice. I am proud of the work they are doing, and it gives me the motivation to keep pushing myself to do more.

Find your VOICE, so students find THEIRS.

Looking at my family background in education, maybe the signs were there all along when I was a child. The way that my parents raised me to see the value in learning, in working hard, and staying focused on constant improvement, I recognize how those experiences shaped me into the educator and the person that I am today. My parents taught me to not give up and to focus on learning first before everything else. Getting a D or worse was okay, but what was not okay was getting that grade because I hadn't prepared well. It was a starting point, and I had to learn from it. My parents taught me that, and they did so by being there to support me and make sure that I could stand on my own. They were deeply invested in my education, and it has made a huge difference in my life. Because of their influence, I have tried to provide the same support for my students.

Teaching Is Awesome

So when did I develop the desire to be a teacher? I'm honestly not really sure at all. All that I am sure of is that teaching was not something that I had ever thought about. It was not part of my plan, and I cannot say that I wanted to be a teacher at all, aside from when I played school as a kid. Thinking back to my college years when it became clear that education was the path I was headed on, I was not entirely convinced then either. I guess we just really never know where our path will lead us, which means that we have to stay open to new ideas and experiences. Even today, I share the story with my students that, had someone told me that I would become a teacher, especially a Spanish teacher, I would never have believed it. It always makes for a great discussion about keeping our options open and not being afraid to take some risks with learning.

About fourteen years ago, I started to rethink what I had been doing in my classroom and became more invested in doing better than I had been. So this might come as a bit of a shock, but I honestly became passionate about being a teacher only about five years ago. Of a career that spans twenty-five years, I can only say I have been fully invested in the last five of them. Now when people ask me why I became a teacher, I'm okay with letting them know how I got into the profession in the first place. But I have a way better answer now than I did back then. It is not just a job with an income. I have found my why. It just took me a little bit longer than it may for most people, but I am clear on it now.

I strive to be a mentor, a role model, a risk taker, and ultimately a person that students and colleagues can count on. I want to be someone who will be there to listen, support, and not judge—someone who will also push back, because that's what we need to do and what we need for others to do to help us grow. My *why* is to make a difference.

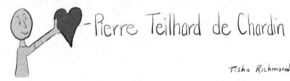

The most satisfying thing in life is to have been able to give a large part of one's self to others.
-Pierre Teilhard de Chardin

Tisha Richmond

Paul O'Neill, Educator, New Jersey @pauloneill1972

Our why dictates our way. A clearly conceived why illuminates the path of our purpose. When our purpose is clear, we become ready to ensure that our daily actions support our mission and vision. Many educators enter the field hoping to make a difference in the lives of children. While this purpose is noble, it is not clear enough. We must understand the needs of each student before attempting to make a difference. This means we must earn an invitation to students' hearts before attempting to enter their minds. This invitation is called trust. When an educator becomes trusted, new pathways become accessible. With consistent reflection, our why can be examined from a variety of perspectives. Our why can be refined and developed over time. A clear why leads to limitless possibilities.

●●●

People Remember How You Made Them Feel

When the news was shared that I was going to write this book, I received so many supportive messages on the different social media platforms. Family members and friends from high school and college, and even people I have never met in person, took the time to congratulate me and send along messages of encouragement. Mindy, one of my high school friends whom I have not seen more than a few times since we graduated, posted a response on Facebook. She answered a question I had long been asking myself: How did I treat others in high school?

We went to elementary school together, and in high school we were both members of the track team. Even though we did not hang out much, we've always been able to pick up and have fun thinking back to those good old days in track. These are the words that really touched my heart.

"Wow! I knew you were a shining star in high school. I just didn't know how bright you shine. I also knew you are an unconditional person; no matter what you did or what group you were in, you never treated anyone different. You were friends with everyone. I was not popular, but you made me feel popular because you were my friend. I can see how you are an amazing teacher because you love unconditionally. Keep shining, my friend! You are amazing!!!"

Reading her comment helped me at a time when I needed a bit of a boost. I don't know if other people, at some point, kind of question what they're doing and where they are in life. Or maybe it's just me, because I'm the type of person who always needs to be pushing myself and pushing the limits in some way. There are days where I feel defeated, that I am not making a difference, that I missed an opportunity to help someone, and that I am not doing enough. I often question why I keep taking on more and not settling for time to relax.

My answer? I want to be able to help others, and so I keep looking for ways to grow. There are times when I feel like I have everything under control, at least moderately, but then I let myself get too comfortable and slow down, but only briefly. However, early on in the 2018–2019 school year, I was feeling like I had lost a bit of my edge and my relevance and didn't feel like the same person I was the year before. The prior school year felt like my best year of teaching yet, and at the start of the new year, I started to again question what I was doing. Mindy's post came at the right time and really mattered to me for several reasons.

I was glad to have our friendship then and now. I had always hoped that I was kind to others and didn't exclude anyone. As a child, I was often the one excluded and sometimes felt that I did not belong. We learn from our experiences, and because of this, I strive to make sure that this does not happen in my classroom. Mindy's message reminds me that even the slightest interactions matter; long after you leave school and move on through your life, people will still remember how you treated them. Every moment matters. We need to make every moment matter for our students.

> Kind words can be short and easy to speak,
> but their echoes are truly endless.
> —Mother Teresa

Questions for Reflection

1. When did you realize that you wanted to be an educator? Were you inspired by a teacher?
2. What roles do you see yourself in besides being a teacher or mentor?
3. What are your strengths, and how did you develop them?

Share your why by tweeting to the hashtag #FUTURE4EDU.

Chapter 2

RELATIONSHIPS ARE EVERYTHING: MOMENTS, MEMORIES, AND MOTIVATIONS

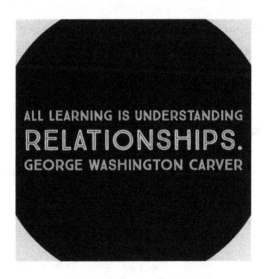

Rodney Turner, Virtual Educator, @TechyTurner, RTEC
Relationships drive so much of what happens in the world. We can see it in nature through the plants and animals. We can even see how relationships drive us as humans. When I think of "relationships," these are my thoughts:

Respecting all people because they are different from you

Encouraging others with smiles, kind words, and things that feed your soul

Loving the small moments of happiness with family and friends

Always being attentive to the feelings of others

Thinking about future repercussions before speaking out of anger or negative emotions

Including the seemingly unlovable—they need it too

Operating your own emotions and actions

Naming the people who bring their perspective to your journey; keep your eyes open.

Share, share, and then share some more—those who love the sharing will stay with you

Having a plan when no one else knows what to do

It starts with you and ends with you

Pursue understanding people, their words and actions, before wanting to be understood

Seek what is right for all people and stay on that path

•••

In education and in life, everything truly comes down to the relationships. It's not something that I really ever thought about when I first started teaching. My focus was only on providing instruction for the students in my classroom and opening lines of communication between us. But over time I started to realize there were other people who needed to be included.

Whether we are classroom teachers, administrators, parents, or community members, we are all connected. What we have in common is wanting and doing what's best for the students in our schools. But it is not just limited to the students in our classes. As teachers, we must invest in all students as we prepare for our future. The most important thing that I think we need to focus on, regardless of our role within the school community, is understanding our relationships and responsibilities to one another. We have to find effective ways to communicate and build a solid foundation that becomes stronger every day. The only way this is possible is if we all strive to learn about and make time for the people in our community. Everyone should be represented and feel valued. We must be willing to keep working at it, even when there are setbacks; we cannot let ourselves feel defeated. Building rapport and relationships takes time.

The Beginning: Knowing Those We Serve

We don't always know the stories of our students and their families. Unless we make time to engage in conversations, be observant, and work on building a connection, we risk missing opportunities to fully support our students and their families. Being an educator carries with it responsibilities beyond just teaching the content; it's about relationships.

It took me a long time to understand the importance of building relationships. Now I work at it each day and focus on it more than the content I am teaching. I would be lying if I said it was easy. Sometimes it is, and other times it takes a while until you feel a connection, build trust, and find common ground. There might even be times when you are ready to give up because you feel like you've exhausted every possible idea to engage with that one student or family, and you don't know what to try next. I have been there, and many times it took greater effort than I imagined. At times it became uncomfortable: frustrated students, unhappy parents, and a teacher who sometimes did not handle things well. We make mistakes and have to own them, and that can feel awkward, but only if we don't work through it. We can't give up, even if the struggle seems too difficult and the challenges feel insurmountable. There is always a way. It's just that it's not always easy.

Thinking about the role that relationships play and those that I have formed the past couple of years, I see the impact on personal learning and student growth. When I reflect at the end of each day, I think about the interactions I had and the progress that I made with students. Sometimes I think about what I could have said or done differently, because what I did just did not work as I thought it would. There have been times during class when I reacted to the behavior first, without taking a moment to pause and see the student and not the behavior. Relationships enable us to see the student first, and the power of reflection helps us to consider how we could have handled the behavior better.

It's not just about making those connections with students; it's also about the relationships that we form with colleagues and other educators. For me, these are people who play an important part in my everyday learning and support system. My hope is that all educators would strive to make relationship building a part of their daily practice, if it is not so already. This is something I wish I had known when I started teaching. During roughly the first fifteen years of my teaching career, there were not too many times when I could say I had built solid and supportive relationships. I can narrow it down to probably only two or three times when I really felt a connection with students and colleagues. The problem was me, keeping myself in isolation and only focusing on teaching the *content* and not the *students*. I was focused on covering the curriculum, assigning homework and tests, and not focused enough on meeting the needs of my students. After recognizing and then accepting that I needed to change, I can see the difference that it made for the students and for me, and it gave me a starting point from which to build.

The strength of our student relationships makes the difference in translating our passion for teaching into their passion for learning.

—Beth Morrow, educator

Kristen Nan, Educator, Pittsburgh, Pennsylvania, @nankr1120
I believe in my heart that the key to learning is a strong foundation built upon relationships fueled by personal passions, and also understanding one another. Regardless of the concept or the people, learning is based on the relationships you create with people and the spark that is ignited between them and their learning.

I build strong foundations by meeting people where they are at in their lives, through their own passions and purpose. If learning is to truly resonate then it must have meaning. The kind of meaning that speaks to a person's soul, the kind that is built beyond words. This kind of learning moves forward and opens up opportunity through voice and choice. There is an instant connection between a person and learning when it is amplified by personal interest. It's the moment someone's ears perk up and he or she starts nodding in agreement. It is that very moment they forget that anyone else is in the room, and the connection is being made solely for them as it resonates deep within their mind and heart. Understanding one another opens doors to building stronger relationships and leads each of us to endless amounts of learning.

●●●

I think we just need thoroughly different relationships.
—Seymour Papert, "Future of School," 1982

Seymour Papert, renowned computer scientist, mathematician, and educator, known for his constructionist theories of learning and learning by doing, pushed thinking when it came to education. He was originally laughed at when he shared his visions for the future of learning and how computers would become an integral part of education. He strongly emphasized the value in relationships. I came across his quote, made thirty-six years ago, and wondered why we are just starting to realize the importance of relationships and their impact on learning. Educators are disrupting the traditional classroom structure to redefine the relationships from within the classroom. We are leveraging technology to enable us to build relationships beyond the classroom. Perhaps this is what Seymour Papert was envisioning.

Over the last five years, I have learned the value of building relationships and have reevaluated the why behind their importance. The power of technology enables us to do so much: give a voice to those who don't speak, share ideas in a comfortable and often anonymous way, provide access to a world of learning, and connect on a global scale. To get a better understanding of what educators from different backgrounds and experiences think about education today, I created a survey related to teaching and professional development. I wanted to know what educators considered to be the most important issues, responsibilities, and needs in education today. A common theme emerged from over 350 responses: building relationships.

Most of the respondents indicated the need to focus on building relationships and getting to know students from the very beginning of the year and working on it daily. Don't wait until some time in the future, because the future is now. Take every moment and make it matter. Build in activities to help the students connect with one another and to feel comfortable connecting with you. Start with community and know the students personally as well as academically. Spend time making those connections; let them get to know you, understand why you teach, and see your passion for what you do. Students who know that they are cared for and truly matter beyond what they are learning in the classroom will be more invested. When students feel valued as people and contributors to the design of the classroom, it has a positive effect on their learning potential and sense of belonging.

Redefining Who We Are:
Be a Champion for Students and Learning

We need to take time to think about our roles as educators and what that means in classrooms today. Are we "just teachers" and only concerned with the delivery of content knowledge? Or has "educator" expanded to include other roles such as mentor, counselor, coach, encourager, and role model, to name a few? Sometimes students count on their teachers as much as they would a parent: there is a strong connection built upon trust that develops. There are many other roles that educators have, but I think that one of the most important roles is being a mentor.

We are often called upon to mentor the students in our classrooms, as well as the colleagues in our schools. Throughout our lives, we have mentors. There are times that our mentors have been chosen for us, or sometimes the mentorships simply formed on their own. How many mentors have you had in your life? How many times have you served as a mentor to a student, a colleague, or a friend? How often has it been just by chance that you kind of fell into a mentorship? Think about the impact of these mentorships on you personally and professionally. Was there a supportive connection, or did you feel that you did not have the support you needed? It's important to take time to evaluate your own experiences to help guide you to become a better and more effective mentor for others.

Mentors serve an important part of our lives. We have mentors in our profession, within our families and groups of friends, and through other activities that we may involve ourselves in with our schools or in our communities. How many of your own mentors have been colleagues in your building, from a nearby school community, or within your PLN? Mentorships lead to new opportunities, better relationships, and authentic personal and professional development. If you are not connected, find a way to form your own PLN today. As someone who spent a lot of time in isolation for many years, I cannot emphasize enough what a difference being connected has made for me and for my students.

> One looks back with appreciation to the brilliant teachers,
> but with gratitude to those who touched our human
> feelings. The curriculum is so much necessary raw material,
> but warmth is the vital element for the growing plant and
> for the soul of the child.
>
> —Carl Jung

Think back to your own teachers. How many would you categorize as "just a teacher," meaning they delivered the content but made very few personal connections, and it was like a "transaction" rather than anything personal at all? Did you feel comfortable and supported asking for help, or did it feel awkward, as if it showed a sign of weakness or made you fear negative feedback? How many of your own teachers would you classify as mentors, counselors, coaches, or encouragers? What difference did having that support make for your personal growth? Now think about where you fall in comparison. Are you "just a teacher"? Or are you more invested, by supporting and nurturing the growth of each student, working to develop an understanding of how to best provide authentic and unique learning experiences to each student in your care? What kind of teacher do you wish you had? Be that teacher.

Teachers need mentors too. How many mentors have you had, and what has the impact been on you personally and professionally? And beyond that, have you become inspired to serve as a mentor to someone else? In your own experience, who has been the best mentor for you, and what has that person taught you? I have been fortunate to have supportive mentors who have helped me to grow professionally and taught me what it means to be a mentor. These relationships are so important, because it is through mentorships that we continue to learn and grow and become a better version of ourselves.

Think of a time when you have been the mentor. What could you have done better? Can you identify some changes you experienced from this relationship that had a positive impact on you and those you mentored as well?

Now think about your experience as a student. Which teachers did you appreciate during your years in school and why? What will your students remember about you, long after they have forgotten the content you taught? What will your legacy be?

> The children you teach may not remember you when they get older, but they will always have a part of you inside of them . . . the part that gave them hope and love and taught them to believe in themselves.
>
> —Marlyn Appelbaum

Maureen Hayes, K–6 Humanities Supervisor, Lawrence Township Public Schools, @mhayes611

What do you remember about elementary school?

I remember the smell . . . the smell that would envelop me each time I entered the building. I don't know exactly what that smell was, but I believed it to be a combination of construction paper, glue, books, and maybe even the concoction that was used to clean the floors each evening. I remember going back to my elementary school as a college student, and upon entering, the first thing I noticed was that smell. It brought me right back to kindergarten.

What are the memories that float to the surface whenever I think back?

Well, here are mine . . .

Big books in kindergarten and the excitement of wondering what adventures Miss Bailey would share from the characters of Alphabet Island.

Third-grade plays. We did two that year with Mrs. Smith: The Mystery of the Gumdrop Dragon and another math mystery.

In fourth grade, Mrs. Adams guided us as we built a tepee in the classroom out of two-by-fours and bulletin board paper. We were able to read inside it if we were lucky enough to get first choice of reading spots for the day.

Also in fourth grade, we used milk cartons to create puppets and then wrote and performed plays in groups. We even got to design the scenery for our productions.

In fifth grade, we actually got to publish our writing into books! This was not a common practice in the '70s, and I was so excited to not only write but illustrate and publish my stories with Mrs. Gerrity.

Finally, I remember all of the books. Where I went to school, students had the chance to read every day. Not just the books we were assigned as a "bluebird" or "robin," but also our own self-selected books from the class or school library, and even books we brought in from home. SSR time was our choice time for reading.

When I look at the things that inspired and left me with lasting memories of my early schooling, nowhere do I mention tests, homework, textbooks, or book reports. In fact, the things I enjoyed most were times when I had student choice through my reading, writing, spots for reading, and creating.

I remember the relationships and how my teachers made me feel. Mrs. Adams bought our entire class McDonald's one day for lunch!

I remember teachers who made me feel special, teachers who I know cared about me.

My walk down memory lane reinforced what I already know is best for kids and their success in school:

It's all about relationships.

It's all about student voice and choice.

It's all about student engagement.

●●●

Teaching in Isolation: Why We Need to Break Out

Teaching can become such an isolating profession. Our priority is, of course, to do what's best for our students. But doing our best means we need to be at our best. Often we may find ourselves lacking the time to work with our peers and get the support that we need as well. Without support and time to collaborate, we can burn out. We can lose our passion for the work that we do and replace it with frustration. There is so much that goes into the planning of each day, leaving little, if any, time for us to take a break and connect with colleagues. During any extra time found between classes, we likely make ourselves available to greet students in the hall, and during planning periods we may choose to stay in our rooms so students can find us if they have questions. Teachers can easily become isolated in their own rooms and schools, connecting with peers only in brief moments when moving through the building or arriving to and leaving from the school. Knowing this, what can we do that will not only help us to break free from this isolation but enable us to create additional learning opportunities for our students?

> The most valuable resource that all teachers have is each other. Without collaboration our growth is limited to our own perspectives.
> —Robert John Meehan

We have to connect and build our own networks, even if that means having a small group that communicates through email or text messages, or by using one of the social media tools available. It isn't so much about having those in-person times to collaborate, although time together in the same space is always a plus, but rather it's about the *presence* of others. We need a network to learn from and grow with and rely on for support. A network that will be there to lend an ear and to help us build our skills. Networks are a way to escape our isolation and a place to share frustrations without judgment. Today it is tremendously important—I would even go so far as to say critical—that all educators become part of a PLN (personal or professional learning network). George Couros says, "Isolation is a choice educators make." We need to make a different choice.

You might wonder, *Why do I need a PLN when I can talk to the colleagues in my building during lunch or planning periods?* Ideally that happens, but realistically, think about how many times a day or week that you see colleagues. How often do you find time for conversations? I teach in a small school, and there are many days when I don't even see my colleagues next door, and as for those who teach in other parts of the building, sometimes weeks pass before we see each other. It just does not happen. We spend time in our classrooms, trying to be present in our doorways and interacting with our students. However, this leaves very little time, if any, for our colleagues. The time with our students is critical for building a solid foundation, but we also need to find time for our own supportive network.

Lack of time is always a struggle. One of the many benefits of using technology to become connected is that it magically creates more time. How? Technology is not always the answer, and it is not a true substitute for face-to-face conversations, but it offers a way to escape that isolation we might be feeling. We can connect virtually through social media or web tools that promote anytime collaborating and communicating. But we have to take that first step out of our isolation.

Melissa Pilakowski, an educator that I met through a Twitter chat, shared her experience with becoming a more connected educator and the impact on her and her students.

Melissa Pilakowksi, @mpilakow

Expanding my network of colleagues opened my world. Until then, I'd been limited to seeing and hearing what my local colleagues did in their classrooms. I compared myself with them, strove to be more like them.

Twitter introduced me to hundreds, then thousands of other teachers who used different methods with different approaches, who challenged my thinking about assessments, room design, student choice and input, and most of all, relationships. My PLN on Twitter helped me grow. I realized I didn't need new lessons, tech tools, or classroom management techniques. I needed to be open to my students and give them voice and choice. I needed to build relationships.

●●●

Be strong enough to stand alone, smart enough to know
when you need help, and brave enough to ask for it.

—Ziad K. Abdelnour

My friend Elizabeth Merce, an educator and member of the #4OCFPLN (a PLN that grew from a book study of *The Four O'Clock Faculty* by Rich Czyz) is passionate about the value of being connected and in showing vulnerability. Elizabeth advises:

> What is one of the best ways to stand alone, know your own limits, and have the courage to ask for help? Develop a diverse professional learning network (PLN). What do I mean by a diverse PLN? Find others who teach different subjects or grade levels or have roles that vary from yours in some way. Seek educators who have different levels of experience. Include educators from different geographical regions and varied settings (public, private, urban, rural, suburban). Diversity in your PLN ensures that you have a variety of viewpoints, experiences, and expertise to draw from when you need help. It also means you can build up your self-efficacy as you act as a support for others.
>
> A good PLN will allow you to be vulnerable. They will allow you to shine. They will help you to better understand yourself and others. They will be there through this journey, and for that there is no replacement.
>
> Where can you find these educators? What tool can you use to connect to other educators? The answers to this lie within yourself. What platforms are you most comfortable with? Twitter, Instagram, Voxer, Facebook, and Periscope already have great net-

works where you can connect to other educators. If you already have personal accounts on a platform, start up a professional one and try searching hashtags that interest you. Comment on, like, and share material that you like. Reach out and send messages to educators that share similar philosophies or challenge you to think. The first platform you use may not be the best one for you, so keep trying! I found my lifeline in Voxer, a platform I had only been using for a month. Who would have thought that trying out a new platform would lead to the best connections of my life (beside my husband of course!).

●●●

As educators, we owe it to our students to provide the best learning opportunities we can for them, and that means doing whatever it takes to be at our best. We can no longer do this in isolation. While reading *Social LEADia* by Jennifer Casa-Todd, a quote from Mark Carbone and Donna Fry caught my attention: "Connected learners need connected leaders."

This quote serves as my reminder of the importance of becoming part of a learning network. Whether it is connecting with colleagues within your school, or connecting virtually with colleagues from around the world, there are so many ways to bring a world of learning to our students and to ourselves. We are better together. I am better today than I was yesterday because of a supportive PLN and a newfound willingness to take risks, fail, and try again.

If I could offer one word of advice to a new teacher or to a teacher who might be going through some challenges, reach out to your colleagues, find a network to connect with, and see what a difference it makes in your personal and professional life. My hesitancy to connect on any social media platforms and my habits of isolating myself in my room or in the teacher work center did not help me to find my way, and being connected for a few years has made a huge difference for me and for the ways I can enhance the learning experience for my students. There are a lot of options, but you need to choose what works for you and your comfort level. Joining communities like ISTE or a state affiliate organization creates even more possibilities to be involved; stay current with educational trends and best practices; and have access to learning events like webinars, conferences, book studies and more. Tools like Twitter, Voxer, Facebook, or Slack provide access to thousands of resources instantly. At first it can feel strange, communicating and forming friendships virtually. Sometimes people just don't get it, wondering if these "Twitter friends" really exist. How can we share so much with our "virtual friends"? But there is such power in connecting and collaborating in this way. We have to put ourselves out there to share our ideas and gather new ones, build on our strengths, and seek help for areas in which we need to grow. We can't possibly know everything, but with the power of a PLN, we have opportunities to get whatever we need, when we need it. It just takes one tweet, one post, one vox to connect. Start connecting today: follow the educators who shared their stories in this chapter.

QUESTIONS FOR REFLECTION

1. Have you felt isolated as an educator? What have you done to break free?
2. How have you become a connected educator? What are the positives that you have noticed?
3. How would you encourage a colleague to begin building a PLN? What are some benefits that you would share?

Share it out using the hashtag #Future4EDU.

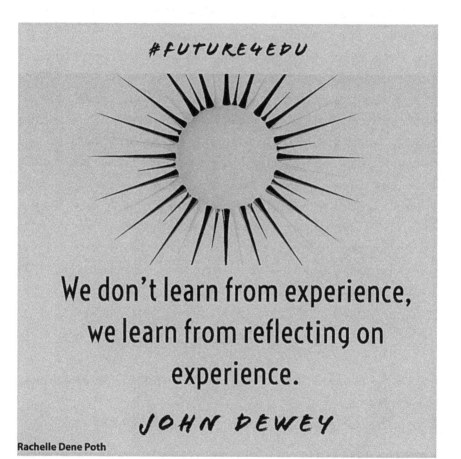

Chapter 3

LEARNING OUR WEAKNESSES

> If people knew how hard I had
> to work to gain my mastery, it
> wouldn't seem so wonderful at all.
> —Michelangelo

To everyone else, it may seem that we have everything under control. We are supposed to be well prepared, have all of the answers, and keep up with all of the changes happening every day. Our lives are supposed to be magically balanced. But let's be real for a minute. It is not always like this; in fact, I find it a rarity. Personally, I am sometimes scrambling at the last minute to pull an activity together, or I don't know the answer to a question and have to look it up, or I handle a behavior issue poorly. I do the best that I can, but sometimes I fail and the students see it. Sometimes my reactions are not the best and I show frustration or defeat. When this happens, there are two choices: (1) try to hide it and push through, or (2) involve students by sharing what happened and what we were hoping for, and work through it together. We have to keep in mind that if we truly want to help students develop the skills that will carry them through in the future, some of those skills are problem solving, quick thinking, and the art of reflecting on mistakes. Part of learning through mistakes is also building social-emotional learning skills. Students need opportunities to collaborate, focus on self-awareness, and develop empathy for others. We provide these opportunities by sharing who we are.

If our students and colleagues don't ever know that we struggle or are going through a rough time in our lives and see how we rise above, we miss an opportunity to connect and develop these skills together. Without showing who we are, and exposing our vulnerabilities, we lose the chance to share a piece of what makes us who we are. Sharing our purpose and passion will help

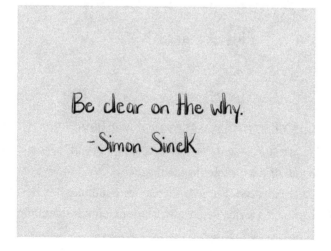

Be clear on the why.
-Simon Sinck

those we work with to understand us better and to foster meaningful connections. Our struggles may be what define us and how we have developed our own skills. There is such power in sharing our stories. Even if it helps just one person, that makes a difference, and the inspiration and lesson learned will be passed to others. The impact on one can lead to an impact on many. We become stronger together.

Elizabeth Merce, Kindergarten Teacher, Virginia Beach, Virginia, @EMercedLearning

The quotes from Michelangelo and Sinek may seem unrelated. They don't appear at the outset to have an obvious connection, but to me they interweave perfectly.

Social-emotional learning "is my jam" as the young kids would say. I have often heard people say that guiding social-emotional learning must come naturally. Those same people say that building relationships is hard, if not impossible, with all students. What if I told you that it isn't easy? What if I told you it wasn't a natural skill? What if instead I told you that social-emotional learning and relationships are actually my weakest area?

You see, I have an ACEs (Adverse Childhood Experiences) score of nine. I was raised by a mother with a score of nine who was raised by a mother with a score of nine. In case you were wondering, ten is the highest. I realized from an early age that the way relationships were formed around me was not "normal."

I decided I wanted more. I wanted to be better and do better for my students and my future family. That became and remains my driving why. I began intentionally studying relationships and social-emotional development. Through intentional study, practice, and reflection, it now appears that I am approaching mastery in the social-emotional domain. The truth is harsher—my why fuels my intense drive to grow.

My story is not uncommon, if you take a moment to listen to those around you. The why that drives us often leads us to devote time, energy, and focus in order to improve. The stronger your why, the more intense you become. Being clear on your why leads to mastery. Find your why. Clarify it. Immerse yourself in it. Develop mastery.

●●●

A failure is not always a mistake, it may simply be the best one can do under the circumstances. The real mistake is to stop trying.

—B. F. Skinner

We can't predict which of our experiences with failure might benefit someone now or in the future. Making mistakes and experiencing failures are often viewed as such negative events. Without a doubt, they can be difficult to work through, and you don't feel so great going through it either. Nobody likes to fail, especially after giving something full effort. But it's time to think about failures in another way.

Think of a time when you took a chance on something, whether you've applied for a job, entered a competition, or taken a test, or any time you've put yourself out there, especially if you had doubts from the start. How did you feel when you either did not do as well as you had hoped or you were not chosen for something? Thinking of my personal experiences, my guess is that you might have felt defeated, afraid to try and possibly fail again. Rejection stings, and if we don't work through it by reflecting and trying again, then we

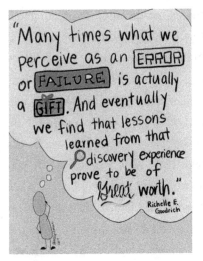

"Many times what we perceive as an ERROR or FAILURE is actually a GIFT. And eventually we find that lessons learned from that discovery experience prove to be of great worth."

Richelle E. Goodrich

will not be the best model for risk-taking and the development of a growth mindset for our students. Rejection can impact us deeply. The feeling of being rejected can be long-lasting. It hinders our motivation for trying again and can lead us to disengage because of the fear or aversion to being rejected again. We can't let this happen. If we do, it will continue to negatively impact our confidence and potential for success. And worse, it will impact our students.

Failures and Their Impact

How many times have you given all of your effort and still failed at something? Think of a time when this happened and consider these questions: Did you share your experience with anyone? Or did you keep it to yourself? Why? Focus on why you made your decision. What were the benefits for you and others if you did? Did you try again or just give up? And if you gave up, why? What did you learn from the experience, or what are your thoughts now?

Two years in a row, I applied for leadership roles in two different organizations, even though I felt like I was completely out of my league. There were many times that I had nearly talked myself out of going for it. The applications were lengthy and required letters of support, which meant that I had to tell others that I was applying. I was uncomfortable asking for the recommendation letters, and this discomfort alone almost led me to back out. I felt anxious about others knowing I had applied for something and then later finding out that I was not selected. But I went through with it and pursued these two positions, still considering withdrawing the applications to avoid the letdown I was sure that I would face. Often I talk myself out of something as a way to prepare for any future disappointment, trying not to get my hopes up too high, even though I do try to be an optimist. Sometimes the doubt gets the best of me. But I followed through and kept hope that I would be selected.

After the rejections came through for both organizations, I didn't think that I would apply again. I had failed, and it really bothered me, mostly because I didn't know where I had fallen short. Did I need to push myself professionally? Were there skills that I could work on to become better? What were my weaknesses? I didn't know. The worst part is that often there is no way to find out an answer to these questions, and so we are left only to our reflections and self-awareness to figure it out. We could compare ourselves with those who are selected and see how our skills measure up with them, but this is not a productive practice. We should not be in competition with anyone but ourselves, and our focus should be on our constant improvement and ongoing progress. Isn't this what we want for our students, for them to take a risk, and sometimes fail, but to keep pushing through, aiming for and ultimately achieving success? What we can do is to reevaluate our qualifications, identify areas of weakness, and try again. The best thing we can do is to let ourselves be vulnerable, reach out to our PLNs, and ask for honest feedback.

Now think about students in similar situations. They have to take tests, try out for sports and activities, enter competitions, apply to colleges, and compete or meet a standard for most everything. How do they feel when they are not successful, either receiving a low grade or not being selected? Do they have an opportunity to learn where they fell short so they can improve? We have to make sure that they do. My own experiences reinforce the importance of giving and receiving feedback. We must actively engage in conversations about areas in which we need to grow, and in so doing, we remind ourselves of the importance of helping our students develop this practice too.

Nobody likes that feeling of not being chosen, whether it's for a classroom activity, a leadership position, or anything that involves an application process. But for me, it serves as a reminder that I need to be okay with failing. Failure means that we have more work to do. Failure means that I tried and have an opportunity to do better.

Failure Means Try Again

I had a year to think about applying again. When the time came, I truly struggled with deciding whether or not I would apply. Again I decided not to ask anyone for advice, partially because of not wanting others to know, and partially because I was intimidated by the possibility of critical feedback (something that I am working on every day). Being okay with receiving feedback does not come easy to me. I have always worried about not being good enough, about not being able to meet an expectation that someone has of me, about falling short. My fear leads me to anticipate the worst sometimes. Throughout my life, I have struggled a lot with self-doubt. Even when others compliment me or say that I did something well, I just do not believe them. It's even difficult to say a simple "thank you" because, in my mind, saying "thank you" implies that I believe what they are saying, and most often I do not. I know there is always room to improve and I am a work in progress.

I have a PLN that I feel comfortable confiding in and trust they will be honest with me. My 53s, a group that I consider to be my closest friends, formed by connecting through social media and conferences. They are my "critical friends," and I trust them completely. But when it came to these experiences, I kept it all to myself again. So I had to rely on my own reflection and assessment of my professional growth to make my decision.

Was it worth trying? Absolutely. Could I handle another rejection? Yes, I thought I could. But I hoped that I wouldn't have to. Had I improved over the past year? Possibly. I decided to apply a second time, but again I received two more rejections. Thinking about it now, I'm not sure if I will apply again. I am very passionate about the work being done by these organizations and want to be involved, but maybe I need to accept that I am just not good enough. *Yet.* And that's okay. But if I give up simply because I failed the first and second time, then it would make me question whether or not I really wanted it at all.

There are lots of people who have failed multiple times and still kept trying. It is usually in the moments when we are ready to give up that things start to shift, maybe just enough to encourage us to keep going, to try once more. But sometimes it is just another setback. And if we don't take chances, then how will we ever really know what we are capable of? Can you think of things that you are good at now, but only after failing many times? What did you do differently? Did you give up or did you keep pushing through?

> Learning is not attained by chance. It must be sought for
> with ardor and diligence.
>
> —Abigail Adams

In preparing for our future and helping students and colleagues, there will be mistakes, failures, and near wins in between. Regardless of what our intended path may be, and how often we get detoured along the way, there is a lesson to learn, and we have the strength to persevere. There will be times when we don't think we are strong enough, and giving up is easier than pushing onward. We can't give up. We must come back even stronger. When we walk with purpose and celebrate these experiences by focusing on the process (growing) and not the product, the lesson we learn and share is that failures are not final. We must model this for those we lead and learn with. Even when the challenges we face seem insurmountable, we get through by sharing our story, pursuing our passion, and learning and failing together.

IF YOU WANT
TO LIFT YOURSELF UP,
LIFT SOMEONE
ELSE UP.
Booker T. WASHINGTON

Understanding Ourselves to Understand Others

Failures, mistakes, and bad days happen to us all. We can let them bring us down, or we can take the energy from the negative feelings and invest it in our students. Sometimes the students are the ones who lift us up. There are days students visit just to talk. It wasn't always this way, maybe a few times when I first started teaching, but then I became disconnected for a long time. After law school and time to re-engage in teaching, the relationships grew, and students started to come into what they call a "welcoming, safe space." I've become better at noticing when something is bothering them. Sometimes this awareness comes through their words, and other times I can see it. I've been there, had struggles with decision-making, and I see similarities in some of my students. Recognizing this self-deprecating behavior has helped me to develop into a more supportive and empathetic teacher. I recognize these qualities in students and try to help them rise above. I strive to be the kind of teacher who promotes risk-taking and is not afraid to share worries, fears, and doubts, because I have had and still have many. My passion is to help others push through whatever might be holding them back. There are times when I still struggle; sometimes it is hard to quiet the voice that tries to talk me out of something. I use my passion for helping others as a way to cast aside my own hesitations. I have learned to lean in and listen.

QUESTIONS FOR REFLECTION

1.   What has to happen for you to move on from a failure? Do you confide in family or friends, or work through it on your own?
2.   What are some strategies to refocus after experiencing multiple failures?
3.   What has been your biggest challenge in your current role, and how have you worked through it? Did you share your story? If not, why?

CHALLENGE

What is the best advice you have received or have given about failures?

Share it out to #FUTURE4EDU.

Chapter 4

GROWING AS AN EDUCATOR AND WHY IT MATTERS

Paul O'Neill

Paul O'Neill, Educator, New Jersey, @pauloneill1972
Asking our students to be accountable for their own learning means that we must hold ourselves as educators to the same standard. Opportunities for professional growth and development are more accessible than ever before. By continuing to grow as educators, we commit to staying up to date with the current trends in teaching and learning. The learning styles of our students continue to evolve at a rapid pace. Growing as an educator is not an option. It is a requirement, necessary to provide our students with the best possible learning experiences and outcomes.

The usage of social media and gaming have led to students seeking instant feedback through a constant culture of approval. These social preferences have extended into our school buildings. How students seek and receive feedback has changed. Gone are the days of writing "Good job" on a student's paper. Today's learners demand more specific feedback. It is our duty to provide them with responses that will motivate them to seek continuous growth.

This level of feedback inspires students to become more curious about their learning. Detailed feedback leads students to question themselves and to reflect on how they can improve on their products as well as their processes.

Some educators may become frustrated when the conversation turns toward growth. The absence of common planning time is cited as a hurdle that stands in the way of professional growth. However, the advent of technology has made professional learning possible any place, anytime, and anywhere. Document sharing, digital conferencing, and distance education allow collegial learning to occur at a convenient time or place. These platforms also allow educators to archive conversations and resources for future reference. These professional portfolios can be shared with others and added to over time.

Educators are reflective practitioners. The most successful educators reflect about their processes as well as their products. They reflect before, during, and after each experience. They learn from every experience regardless of the outcome. They ask questions that require deep reflection. As a result of this reflection, new questions are formed. Deeper levels of reflection become required. These educators ensure that their thoughts and actions are aligned to their mission, purpose, and vision. There are no wasted steps.

Growth-minded educators who learn from their mistakes never settle. They have an unquenchable appetite for improvement. Mistakes become moments that are analyzed with careful scrutiny. Growth-minded educators are constantly searching to create the culture that they desire. In this environment, there are no artificial boundaries. These educators refuse to accept the status quo without carefully examining whether or not these practices are what's best for their students.

My own professional development soared when I began writing every day. I decided to keep a reflective journal that contained thoughts, ideas, and inspiration designed to assist my growth. Once I began writing for a few weeks, a feeling of excitement came over me. I looked forward to getting home so that I could reflect upon the events that took place each day. Soon, I found myself looking back to read previous entries. As I did so, I discovered that new perspectives were developing over time. I was growing from my experiences. I learned that experience provided a platform for growth.

As I continued to grow, I began to ask myself questions.

Would others be interested in my learning experiences?

Would others benefit from my learning experiences?

Where should I publish my reflections?

Would anybody even read my reflections?

One mistake I made during my early days of social media exploration was falling victim to artificial pressure. I set a goal to write every day. My vision was to interact with others through my reflections and experiences. My first attempt at publishing my reflections was met with a modest following, but my goal wasn't to reach millions of people. After writing every day for over six months, I decided to stop. The endeavor was no longer enjoyable. There were days when I felt like I was interacting with only myself. Although my enthusiasm to interact with others was still present, I realized that I wasn't positioned on a social media platform that best suited my pursuits.

However, there was a bright spot. While writing daily, I connected with Kristi Latimer, an equally enthusiastic educator from Texas, who provided me with feedback and challenged me to grow. Soon, the two of us took the plunge and explored the world of Twitter chats together during the summer of 2016. For the next few months, we met other enthusiastic educators and began forming a professional learning network. Over the years, this network continued to grow. Some of these connections would take place weekly, while others would become a part of my daily routine. The Twitter chats were exactly what I was looking for. Each night of the week, various chat topics were being addressed by educators all over the world. Challenges that I currently faced were being discussed. I entered each chat curious to hear how others faced similar issues and hopeful to find solutions that applied to situations I was facing. I left each chat relieved that I was not the only person facing these challenges. I also left each chat feeling excited to apply the new lessons learned to my professional life. In addition, meeting new people from various districts provided me with more opportunities to discuss ideas, goals, obstacles, and barriers.

Each morning, I'm able to receive targeted professional development on my way to work. Using an app called Voxer, I'm able to listen to audio recordings from educators all over the world. These words serve many different purposes. Some mornings they serve as a source of inspiration. Other times, they serve as validation. I've been inspired to create new ideas and initiatives. I've also been encouraged to go back to the drawing board and start from scratch.

The chats were fun . . . well, they still are, but there was something missing. I still had the desire to create content. Since I had already scratched my writing itch, I decided to reflect in a different way. This led to the creation of a hashtag that would center on learning alongside my professional network: #PLN365. The goal was to celebrate growth and development on a daily basis with a group of educators. How this takes place continues to evolve over time. Currently, I record video reflections that are posted on Twitter. This has made meeting other educators very exciting since our virtual connection gives us common ground to discuss when we meet in person. Perhaps the full tale will be told as the subject of my own book someday.

While #PLN365 has experienced greater success on Twitter than my previous social media endeavor, it did not occur without mistakes. Learning how and when to advertise chats was a process. Creating promo posters also required some trial and error. All of this happened before the first chat actually took place. When it was time for the first chat, I was nervous. Would people attend, or would I be interacting with myself once again? The first chat exceeded my expectations. There were great conversations taking place and positive feedback afterward.

Despite the successful debut, there were still growing pains. For quite some time, I focused too frequently on the quantity of people who participated during each chat instead of the quality of the chat itself. A new chapter of the hashtag took place on January 1, 2018. I decided to enter the world of video reflection. Since then, every day has been an experience. I've met many people who have contributed to my professional development. Extending my professional network has immensely contributed to my growth.

As an administrator, I've spoken with many educators about the potential power of social media in education. Some have excitedly embraced the opportunity, while others have remained reluctant. Those who have been hesitant have benefitted from watching their colleagues take the plunge. The best part about putting yourself out there on social media is that your profile does not need to look a certain way. Listed below are some of the various ways educators have used social media to celebrate learning.

- Reflections
- Pictures
- Videos
- Links
- Chats
- Book talks
- Resources
- Blogs
- Hashtags

Extending learning outside the classroom via social media also provides families with a glimpse of what's happening in the lives of their children each day. Conversations at the dinner table now include more details when the question "What did you learn in school today?" is asked. Feedback from families has been overwhelmingly positive. Collaboration between families and our school district has been stronger. Students can now receive more help at home since families have a better understanding of what's going on in school.

Through it all, becoming a connected educator has not only helped me grow but has helped the growth of others as well. One of my favorite strategies is to bring learning back to the educators I work with every day. I encourage those of you who are thinking about connecting with others to take the plunge. Through collaborative efforts, we are truly stronger together.

QUESTIONS FOR REFLECTION

1. How have you grown as an educator since the beginning of your professional career?
2. How can you step outside of your comfort zone in order to grow?
3. What is one way you can assist a colleague who has a fixed mindset?

CHALLENGE

- Challenge #1: Start a growth journal that documents one new lesson learned each week.
- Challenge #2: Grow your professional learning network and help build the learning network for others.
- Challenge #3: Take being a connected educator to another level. Work together with others to organize an Edcamp.

Share it out to #FUTURE4EDU.

Chapter 5

GOAL SETTING FROM VULNERABILITIES AND VICTORIES

My path to becoming connected and developing my own personalized professional learning network surprisingly started with social media. I was not always a fan of it, based on how I saw others using it, and cannot say that I truly saw the value of what each platform might have to offer. Honestly, I just didn't get it. It seemed strange to connect with people in this way. My experience was limited, and my impression was that these platforms were used only for sharing news with family and friends and not for learning—simply social channels that connected people in a different way. But I was wrong. I did not take time to learn about Twitter or Facebook or other platforms, and I had some misconceptions about the benefits of each, which led to my avoidance of using them. My misconceptions were based on the experiences of others rather than judging the value and benefits for myself. I didn't think they could be of professional value. I was breaking my longstanding rule against acting based on the opinions of others rather than judging something based on my own experience.

Bringing the World In: Making a Big World Small

Technology amazes me. Ever since I was a kid, I have loved trying new things, especially when it comes to *tech*. Computers, VCRs, CD players, and even microwaves fascinated me. Even with all of the tools available, I consider one of the most impactful transformations through technology to be the creation of communication tools. Communication in my childhood consisted of making phone calls and getting a busy signal, writing a letter and waiting a week or longer for a response, or passing notes to friends in school and hoping they would "write back soon." So much time spent waiting for someone to respond. We communicate much faster now than I ever thought possible. Now through email, messaging apps, and social media, we can quickly exchange ideas, ask for help, and share resources. I was fine with email and phone calls and figured, why complicate things with social media? I held off on creating Facebook and Twitter accounts because I had the perception that the purpose was simply to give a "life update" and not for professional learning.

I also didn't see any personal benefits of using social media until I had to track down nearly six hundred people for a class reunion. Being realistic, I knew that picking up a phone book (if I could find one) in 2006 would not help much and that I had to explore other ways to find classmates. Eventually I gave in, created a Facebook account, and little by little, sure enough, I realized that I had been *mostly* wrong. Besides tracking down classmates, I found learning communities and other educator groups to join. These virtual spaces evolved into a great way for sharing information and adding resources: amazingly (not that I thought this years ago), a tremendous tool for learning and professional growth. I was amazed at how quickly people could connect with anyone in the world, at any time, yet I hesitated on diving into the social media platforms for so long.

Next came connecting with Twitter, the "Twitterverse" or "Twittersphere." Again, I was wrong about its value for professional learning and believed it was only for celebrities or talking about politics or sports. Hashtags did not make sense to me, and I did not plan to figure them out until a friend tagged me in a tweet. That tweet was the beginning of a learning journey.

Engaging in a New Form of Professional Learning

Giving Twitter a try was interesting. I came across a chat one night and tried to jump right in. Not having any idea what I was doing, I tried to keep up with the "feed" and learn something new. My first chat, *#wileychat*, was with a few people from North Carolina and Tennessee. My path toward becoming a connected educator and finding professional value in Twitter came about by jumping into a chat led by Sean Gaillard, where I also met Julie Daniel Davis, Greg Bagby, and Katrina Keene. From that point on, my interest in and presence on Twitter continued to grow. The potential for professional learning is tremendous, and the best part was meeting them face to face in Philadelphia during the ISTE 2015 conference. By taking a risk with Twitter and stepping out of my traditional and comfortable ways of teaching and learning, I realized the power of being a connected educator and its impact on students and those we lead.

Take a few moments to think about everything we are capable of today. With these two social media platforms alone (ones which I adamantly avoided), tremendous possibilities for learning and connecting exist, creating opportunities to provide more for our students than ever before. Realizing I was wrong helped me to learn a valuable lesson: in order to really understand something, you have to investigate it *yourself*. You have to take a chance, take a risk, and try something before making any judgments. (This is a very important lesson for life as well.) And of course, you shouldn't just start using something because everybody else is. We are all so uniquely different. I've always told my students that we can all read the same book but get a different story. Experience things for yourself first and then decide.

BUILDING
RELATIONSHIPS
MEANS
SHOWING
VULNERABILITY

Vulnerability in Learning:
Why We Shouldn't Hide Our Weaknesses

What if no one ever spoke up when they needed help? If every effort was made to keep areas of weakness or struggle hidden from others, how would we be able to help our students or colleagues if we didn't know? How could others help us if they didn't know? We need to communicate and we need to be observant. It might be a look on someone's face, body language, or another way of manifesting discomfort when it comes to what is being covered in class or maybe even just dealing with life in general. We all struggle, and as educators, most likely we don't let others know. Aren't we supposed to maintain a positive presence and keep whatever we might be dealing with outside of our classrooms and leave our personal struggles at home? I think that the perception has always been yes. We are supposed to be the experts, the strong leaders, the people who create a positive, supportive, and welcoming learning space for others. From the outside looking in, it might seem that we always know exactly what we are doing: we have the skill set needed to get through any challenge, and it might even seem like things come easy to us in our role as educators. But we know that is not always true.

We are human, we have our own personal challenges, and sometimes it can be hard to separate those from our teacher personas. But do we really need to? Should we always portray that we live a life without struggle? Or is it okay to share moments of weakness, to show our vulnerability? I think it is. Showing our true selves, being transparent, honest, and open about who we are, is important for creating a culture of concern, kindness, and empathy.

When we give ourselves permission to fail, we, at the same time, give ourselves permission to excel. ~ Eloise Ristad

Failing as a Teacher: Experiencing Defeat

My teaching career started in 1994 when I began working as a substitute after graduating from Penn State. I was so nervous at first, but the nerves calmed after spending a few days in schools. Maybe it was the comfort in knowing I was only there day to day without the full responsibility of a regular teacher. Maybe it was because I didn't teach in the same class and did not have a personal investment in the students I was teaching. It was not that I didn't care; I did. But they were not *my* students. For three years of working as a substitute, I enjoyed my everyday variety of teaching different classes, grades, and even in different schools. Being a substitute gave me flexibility without all of the responsibilities while I worked toward my Spanish certification. I hoped that an additional certification would open up new job opportunities, but part of me wanted to keep my flexible schedule because I still lacked passion about being a teacher.

I enjoyed being in the classroom, but for some reason I had decided that I would place myself on a "ten-year plan" once I found a permanent position. I could see myself teaching for about ten years, although I had no idea of what I would do instead. I think part of me had dreams of something bigger than teaching. I just didn't know what that was . . . yet. And part of me wished that someone would just tell me what I should do so I did not have to make any big decisions. Fear of making the wrong decision continues to be a struggle. The type of decision has no bearing on my indecisiveness, as even deciding something simple like what or where to eat for dinner is more than I want to think about on some days.

Failing at Fitting In

When I started a part-time, long-term substitute position, I did not have a classroom to call my own. I had three very different classrooms for the three classes that I taught. One was a computer lab where I couldn't always see what the students were doing. One was a classroom without doors where the noise traveled between classrooms and students writing on the board could slide the chalk along the tray to the classroom next door and disturb that class. One was a small room in the library for a multi-level Spanish class. I traveled upstairs and downstairs, which often made me late to classes and impacted my preparation. Students were unsupervised until I arrived, making it difficult to get them to focus and to establish a consistent routine. This definitely made my job a bit more challenging, because there was no consistency in the space that I was using for my classroom. From the outside looking in, I am sure it seemed that I had no control, and that is probably pretty accurate.

Aside from these challenges, I didn't have the greatest background in teacher preparation from my undergraduate courses, so I didn't know how to balance lesson preparation and classroom management. Several educators in my PLN currently work with pre-service teachers, and their programs are providing the right learning opportunities and supports for the future teachers, and preparation which I lacked as a new teacher many years ago. Dr. Sam Fecich, a professor at Grove City College, created a tremendous program full of enriching professional learning experiences for pre-service teachers. My own experience was not as structured, so I didn't know how to handle discipline or how to set up a structure that worked. Not having my own classroom where I felt comfortable and could establish my authority did not help either. Teaching in someone else's room always made me nervous because I worried that students might interfere with the teacher materials, and I didn't have time to get things ready on the board before students came in. Thinking back now, maybe part of it was that I was not fully invested. Some days I was just trying to make it through and go home.

When I started my full-time teaching position, it was not how I had imagined it would be. The realization of the huge amount of responsibility that goes along with being a classroom teacher hit me. What had I gotten myself into and how long would I last? Maybe I had seen one too many movies about teaching and expected classrooms, students, and teachers to be exactly like they were portrayed in the movies. They were not. Some days I wanted to go back to working as a substitute, because those days were easier to get through. In my full-time job, some things frustrated me early on, and there were days when I left school feeling totally defeated and alone.

I felt overwhelmed by the number of different courses that I was teaching and the number of students in each class. I also did not have my own classroom for the first two years, so I traveled and lugged my materials from room to room. There were struggles with classroom management and connecting with the students. Dealing with behavior problems, trying to get students to work, and balancing a full schedule were all new to me. There was a lot to deal with between student behaviors and my lack of organizational skills. Sometimes I drove home dreading going back the next day. It was tough and I did not know how to make it better. And part of me back then did not want to try.

NO ONE SHOULD TEACH WHO
IS NOT IN LOVE WITH TEACHING.
MARGARET E. SANGSTER

I was not in love with the "job." I felt like I couldn't do it; it was exhausting, and some days I wanted to give up. I would have gladly gone back to being a substitute or working as a waitress, where every day was different and without as much responsibility. But I tried to do my best, and regardless of my feelings about the "job," I truly wanted to help the students to succeed. I just didn't know how to improve or where to start. Knowing what I know now, I could have done so much more back then, and I should have. I isolated myself because I moved around so much without a space to call my own, and I didn't have time to connect. I kept to myself and should have made time to ask for help, but that would have meant admitting that I wasn't good enough, showing my vulnerability, and I was not comfortable doing that. My intentional isolation impacted more than just me; it limited opportunities for my students.

What if I had asked students for some input and spent more time getting to know them? Would that have made a difference? Inviting students to be co-designers in the classroom and work with them to build our learning community. It would have been easy, simply by greeting them at the door or moving around in the classroom, rather than standing isolated in the front. I think I expected to be the same person I was as a substitute, and I did not know how to make the transition to a full-time teacher. I made a lot of mistakes back then, and I've been a constant work in progress ever since. I finally feel that I have found my way and my why. It has taken a long time, but I have been on a good path of personalized professional learning and development, only because I tried something different. I broke away from isolation, reached out, and became connected. I learned the importance of relationships and of asking for help when I need it. I know that I am meant to be a teacher. I wish only that I had realized it sooner. I was too focused on the job and not what mattered most: my students.

My hope is that my story will help you to make some changes, to connect and lead with confidence. Embrace the power of being vulnerable. We are all learners and always have room to grow.

Learn First, Then Lead: Finding That Passion

I know a lot of educators who are so passionate for teaching and learning. You can feel it when they speak, see it in their body language, and their energy is contagious. They make you want to become a better teacher. Their passion pushes you to think about your practice and how to improve. It's not in their words, but in their actions. I lacked that passion for many years. There were many things that I really enjoyed about teaching, but I never had the same passion as many of my friends and colleagues. It took longer to develop, and I discovered it only after heading back into the classroom as a student. What an impact that had on my passion for teaching.

I think a part of our professional development should include being a student in a physical classroom again. It can help educators to better understand how students learn, gather new ideas, and think about the teaching methods being used in their own classrooms. Educators would benefit by experiencing all components of a class like procedures, assignments, grades, and opportunities for collaborating with other educators. Educators can build skills and become even better teachers by being a student again.

Going back to school after receiving my Spanish degree was something that I wanted to do, but I had not found a program that interested me or that I thought I could do well in. Even as an adult, the fear of failure and self-doubt still affect me. Obtaining a master's degree in French or Spanish was not something I wanted to pursue, and there were no other programs that caught my attention. Indecisiveness has been a lifelong struggle.

A few courses in the Spanish program focused on legal translation, which led me to become interested in law. Having read John Grisham novels in college, I always thought law would be an interesting career, and at one point I considered studying to be a paralegal. A few years passed by, and then, on a whim and after weeks of cramming, I took the LSAT (Law School Admission Test) and decided to apply to law school. I was accepted at the Duquesne School of Law as an evening student for the fall of 2002. Looking back, I did not expect to receive that acceptance letter.

I waited a few days to tell my husband and my parents that I had been accepted. They had no idea that I had applied, or even why, and initially were concerned about the changes ahead for me, but they were very supportive. It was a big decision, a huge time commitment that would be added to my full teaching schedule. Almost entire days would be spent in the classroom, four nights a week for four years. Scared, yes. Terrified, completely. Afraid to fail, definitely. But it was a new opportunity to push myself out of my comfort zone and see what I was capable of, now that I had not taken classes in a few years.

When my law school news started to spread, there were a lot of questions asked and comments made to and about me. I overheard some people saying they weren't sure if I "had what it took to be an attorney." Discussions about whether I "would be able to handle the coursework" took place, and predictions were even followed by laughter. There were comments made directly to me based on the color of my hair with references made to my IQ, suggesting that I was not smart enough because I was a blonde. It made me wonder what these people thought about students and their abilities. As an adult I could take it, but I couldn't believe the judgments, stereotyping, and unkind remarks made so openly. There were assumptions that I wanted to quit teaching and predictions of how soon I would leave. Attending law school was not something I chose to do because I didn't like teaching. I wanted to challenge myself to learn something different and explore new possibilities. People wondered what made me want to go back to school to pursue a degree in an entirely different career while teaching full time. I honestly have no idea, but it was a decision that I had made, and I had no plans of backing out—definitely not after hearing comments aimed at knocking me down before I even started.

Part of my interest in going to law school came from feeling that I hadn't pushed myself enough as an undergraduate. I had taken a light course load and had an easy schedule. I was afraid of failing and disappointing my family and worried that I would flunk out. Back then, still a teenager, I didn't know what I wanted to do. But when it came to the decision to apply to law school,

I went for it. I chose not to tell anyone because it was something that I needed to do for myself. I wanted to know if I had what it took to be accepted. Were my test scores and educational background and experiences enough? I didn't want the day to come when I looked back and wondered what I could have done differently. Keeping it a secret was my way of protecting myself from showing defeat if I failed.

Amy Storer, Instructional Coach, Keenan Elementary School, Montgomery ISD, @techamys

If you look up the definition of failure in a dictionary, it goes a little something like this . . . lack of success. When I think back to my first year as an instructional coach, I see so much growth, but I know that so much of that came with going through failure and doubt. I knew that it would be tough to no longer have students to care for, but I was so excited about starting this new role. I was placed at our fifth-grade campus, and although nervous, I knew that I was being placed there for a reason. It was where I was meant to be. With very little training in the coaching model, I did what all great teachers do. I started with the heart. I worked hard during the first part of the school year to grow and foster strong relationships with the educators I was working alongside.

When I started working with teachers on their goals and action plans for the year, my first mistake happened. I made it all about *me*. If their goal was about meaningful technology integration, I shared all the tools that *I loved*, when I should have listened to what they loved. Recognizing this mistake and failure early on helped with my growth as a coach. I knew almost immediately that I had gone about that the wrong way. So what did I do? I reached out to my PLN, did lots of research, and read many books. I used that "hiccup" as a way to grow as a professional. I could have let this experience stop me in my tracks, but I didn't. I was blessed to work with this first group of teachers and administrators who taught me so much about being an instructional coach. I am forever thankful for their lessons and friendships.

It took me a long time to realize the power in failing. For so many years, when failure occurred in my life, I viewed it as a weakness when I should have viewed it as an integral part of my journey. These important points in my life weren't steps back but steps forward to what I was meant to achieve or experience. Life shouldn't be easy. We should be crawling, walking, and then running toward exactly who we were meant to be. We should be experiencing triumph and struggle. All of the roadblocks and hurdles that are thrown our way are just as much a part of the journey as the smooth and easy paths. Embrace them all.

●●●

Scott Nunes, Teacher at James C. Enoch High School, @MrNunesTeach

I don't like being told what I cannot do in terms of ability. In college, my advisor told me that I should switch majors because I was not cut out for English, which made me angry and just motivated me to push harder! I went to every single office hour offered, received peer and other teacher feedback on my essays, and got an A in my last course with them as a result of my hard work and determination.

In terms of teaching, this has been me digging deep, cranking out hours reading, planning, and preparing for engaging lessons, building my PLN, and exploring new opportunities. One of these opportunities made me really nervous—Minefaire.

I felt that as the days got closer I was bound to fail miserably, but I kept pushing forward—this time not so much due to my own strength, but rather the encouragement of others and their belief in me. The fact that others trusted me with this job propelled me to do an excellent job at it, and I succeeded!

●●●

Your destination might not end up being exactly what you envisioned to start with, but if you stick it out and work through the challenges, what you end up with will be far better than you could have ever imagined. -Joy Mangano

Thirteen years after graduation and passing the bar exam, I am still teaching and have not done much legal work at all. Law school changed who I am as a teacher and a person. I experienced life as a student in different and often uncomfortable learning environments where I struggled and did not believe in myself. I experienced the same discomfort my students might feel when asked questions they don't know the answers to. It was eye-opening because it led me to realize that I had been doing "the job" of teaching. I was teaching like I had been taught, and while that is not necessarily a bad thing, I wasn't considering the individual needs of my students. I taught based on the methods that worked for *me*, not them. I didn't ask my students for any input, and so I could not provide the best learning environment for them. Not having a strong background in pedagogy meant that I was losing the connection and the knowledge base of current teaching methods with every passing year.

Why? Because for a long time I used a lot of the same class materials, lessons, projects, and tests. I kept to myself, choosing to eat lunch alone in my room and work through my planning periods. I was involved with extracurricular activities like being a sponsor for the Spanish club and the color guard instructor, but other than those, I was not working on connecting with students. I kept my "teacher presence" in my "teacher space," and I was okay with doing that every day, year after year, until I became a law student. Professors who pushed my thinking—and one professor in particular, Bruce Antkowiak, who taught us what it means to be an educator and a mentor—inspired me to become a better teacher by being a better student.

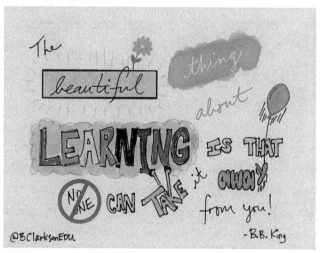

While I'm not truly using my law degree, you can't put a value on learning. Whether or not you apply these skills in your daily life, it is still something that impacts you and can lead to other opportunities in life. There are many lessons I learned from law school that did not come from books.

The greatest lesson I learned was from a professor who not only shared who he was, what he stood for, and whom he fought for, but also taught us the power of telling our stories. I started down a different path as a teacher because of Bruce Antkowiak, and without that experience, I'm not sure that I would still be in education today. For me, it instilled a passion for teaching that I had not yet discovered and an awareness that I needed to see my students, to know who they are so I can be better for them.

> If you're struggling with self-doubt, remind yourself of all of the times you overcame what you did not know.
>
> —Brendon Burchard

Questions for Reflection

1. Have you always wanted to be an educator? How do you share your passion for learning?
2. There will be personal struggles in our lives. What are some strategies for recharging and staying positive?
3. Think about the greatest lessons you have learned from failures. Have you shared your experience with your students? Why is it important to share your failures with them?

Share it out!

What are the best ways to grow a PLN, and why does it matter?

Tweet to #FUTURE4EDU.

Chapter 6

FIND YOUR WHY
AND THEN YOUR WAY

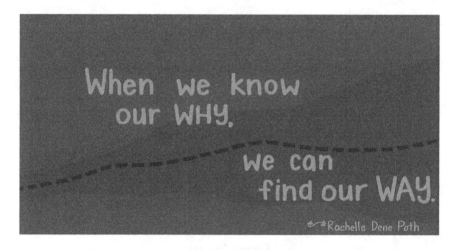

When we know our WHY,

we can find our WAY.

Rachelle Dene Poth

Do you remember the first group of students you taught, the ones who challenged you on occasion, if not often, for whom you may have stayed long after school and worked really hard to make learning a special experience? Were you able to connect and build relationships with them? Or was it a class where, no matter what you tried, you struggled, there were challenges, and the classroom culture just didn't click? For whatever reason, neither you nor they could connect. While we want to find ways to make those connections, we have to think about why sometimes it just does not work.

Maybe it was because you didn't have enough experience, or there wasn't enough effort by you or your students, or they just pushed back too much. Maybe it was a combination of all of these that made it an obstacle in your classroom. It's okay because we learn as we go. Nothing is perfect from the beginning, and if things come too easily then you're not truly learning and growing. Relationship building can be tough and frustrating, but we have to keep working at it because giving up is not an option. Our goal is to help students learn to collaborate and communicate, prepare to work with others in the future, and develop social-emotional learning skills. We need to find a way to get along, to respect one another, even if we don't always agree or even like each other. It happens. The classroom space provides the best opportunity to work on this. Try to identify two or three times during your career when you felt you had really made a difference, made a connection, and classroom culture was positive. Then try to think of a time when it didn't come so easily. What lessons can we learn by reflecting on these different experiences?

EVERY CHILD
DESERVES A CHAMPION-
AN ADULT WHO WILL NEVER
GIVE UP ON THEM,
WHO UNDERSTANDS
THE POWER
OF CONNECTION,
AND INSISTS
THAT THEY BECOME
THE BEST THAT
THEY CAN
POSSIBLY BE

- Rita F. Pierson

@SteinbrinkLaura

The first time I felt a connection was during my very first half year of teaching. I taught three classes: French I, Exploratory French and Spanish IV/V. There were some really challenging days, and I wasn't sure that I would make it for the rest of the year. Student behaviors at times were unpredictable, and I didn't feel as though I was seen as an authority or had their respect. I think part of it was their knowing I was new to the building, coming in mid-year without my own classroom. Some days it definitely was a struggle.

I had students who would give up so easily. They thought the material was too difficult or they lacked confidence when answering. There were times when tears came, or their frustrations came out in anger or led to complete shutdowns. I didn't know how to handle it; I had never experienced student reactions like these before, and my responses were probably not the best. Sometimes I yelled or I took it personally. I reacted in ways that my own teachers had reacted when I was in school, trying to redirect them and stop the behavior rather than listening in to understand the reason for it. All I could see was the behavior interrupting my plans and not the student who needed my attention. If I could do it all over again, I know better now and would do better. But back then, I just thought that the students would respect me and be responsive to me, and that I wouldn't have any problems with discipline or teaching the content. But I did, and it took a while to realize that not all students would get along all the time, that they all didn't learn the same way, that some possibly had negative experiences in school, or difficulties at home, and might be dealing with issues on their own. And I also realized that not every single student would like me or my class. I struggled with the words to say and the actions to take. Not knowing how to help, or if I should, and not being comfortable asking students to confide in me made it difficult to work through. But it was my fault for not trying enough or reaching out to the other teachers. My mistake was keeping myself isolated instead of asking for help. And worse, I was looking at teaching the class and not teaching each student.

A good teacher must be able
to put himself in the place of
those who find learning hard.
˜ Eliphas Levi, French Author

@rishrich

Something had to change, and it had to be me. Thinking back to my student teaching experience, I taught students of varying interests, abilities, and personalities. In several classes I had students who openly voiced their lack of self-confidence and doubts about their abilities and sometimes completely shut down in class. When I tried to help, a few of them pushed back hard and did not want to respond. I kept trying, always wondering if I would be able to connect with them, to get them to trust me and let me help. But after only a few weeks, students started to connect with me, asking me about regular life things like where I went to school, what I enjoyed doing, why I wanted to be a teacher, and other random questions they would come up with. Maybe because I was younger and trying to build relationships, it didn't feel uncomfortable to have these conversations and even laugh with my students. But five years later, I lost sight of what a difference those connections can make.

Somewhere along the way between student teaching and this part-time position, my comfort level changed. I was inflexible, and I thought my whole purpose was just to teach and that was it. But this group of French I students did not let me get away with that for long. With each passing week, we strengthened the culture of our classroom and things started to improve. I went from often dreading the class and worrying about what I might face on any given day, hoping to make it through without any incidents, to looking forward to the class and enjoying the unique student personalities. What made the difference? Perhaps by letting my guard down, showing genuine interest in them, working to understand each student's needs, and making adjustments in my teaching, I had made progress without realizing it. A change to leaning in and listening more. I started seeing the student and not the behavior.

Teaching the Class or Teaching the Student?

When I stopped seeing them as a class with behavioral issues and instead saw them as individual students with individual needs, especially in terms of self-confidence and recognizing their abilities, I made progress. Some challenges came from their peer interactions. I don't think they had a lot of experience working together since they were always sitting in rows, listening to the teacher, and maybe silently struggling with the content but not feeling connected enough to ask for help. We can't assume that students know how to work together simply because they sit together in the same classroom. We need to create opportunities for peer collaboration, to build their confidence in learning and form their own support network.

> Empathy is a choice and it's a vulnerable choice.
> In order to connect with you, I have to connect with
> something within myself that knows that feeling.
> —Brené Brown

I remember hearing students call themselves names, openly doubt their abilities, and sometimes make fun of their peers. Some thought they weren't smart enough, wouldn't answer correctly or do as well as their classmates, so they would shut down. Others lost the courage to respond when classmates would make comments. Seeing this happen reminded me of my own experiences in school and bothered me more than some of the discipline challenges that I faced as a new teacher. It bothered me because I experienced the same thing when I was a student.

Even as an adult, I struggle with doubts about my abilities and sometimes lack confidence that I will be successful, whether in teaching or life in general. It is easier to notice and offer encouragement to others than it is to do the same for ourselves. Knowing the burden it can be on a person's self-esteem and potential for growth, it became my mission to lift students up and find ways to empower them in the classroom. This was another lesson learned in law school. As teachers, we must model that it is okay to try and to make mistakes. By showing who we are, being vulnerable and transparent with our students, we create a supportive and welcoming space for students to learn and grow. I was not always okay with sharing the real me, only the teacher persona; that felt safer.

Students Want to Know You

When the semester teaching position turned into full time, my comfort again shifted. For some reason I thought that I had to turn off the relationship-building switch, and I went back to limiting the conversations and interactions that happened in my classes. I worried only about teaching the content, making sure the students were learning and doing what they needed to do so I could cover the required curriculum. I don't know why I felt that way, maybe because originally I was there only as a substitute, and it felt like I could interact and be "real" with students. However, as the full-time teacher it felt more formal, and I put limits on myself. Partially out of fear, as a younger teacher I wanted to establish authority and set classroom boundaries early on. Everything I had learned and observed told me that this was what I *had* to do.

But in spite of what *my* goals were, students were curious. One thing I've noticed about working in a small school is that students and teachers tend to connect more than in larger schools. The relationships are unique. Having come from a big school myself, these friendly and informal relationships and interactions were a bit awkward for me. I was not accustomed to it, and quite honestly, I didn't understand why students wanted to know so much about their teachers or even hang out and talk after the school day ended. Thinking back to my days in high school, I don't remember asking teachers about their personal interests. There was distance kept between students and teachers. Some teachers shared personal stories that were relevant to the course, and others had children in the school, which created a closer connection with them. But mostly there was a line between high school teachers and students that I thought should not be crossed, and sharing personal interests and experiences was on that line.

My students were very interested in learning about me, and no matter how hard they tried, I wouldn't give a lot of information. I didn't think that it was appropriate or a common practice for teachers. I didn't even want to share preferences for TV shows, music, or anything. When students would ask me something, I would change the question, redirect it, say, "I don't know," or give some generic response. Looking back at how I responded to their questions, I wonder how many opportunities I missed for connecting and building a relationship with a student who needed it the most. I can't change it, but I can use it to guide me moving forward. Now I know better, so I do better.

Thinking back to my own experience as a student, I recall very few teachers who shared personal details. I had a few who talked about their interest in music or movies. One of my favorites was my ninth-grade health teacher, who found a way to relate everything back to John Wayne—not a common practice, but it made her relatable, and somehow it helped us to remember the content better. But that was not the norm.

As a student, although I appreciated when my teachers shared more about themselves, because it helped me to connect better with the content, I did not feel comfortable letting my own students in to understand me. I thought it would interfere with their learning process or possibly be influential in some way. Everything that I had learned about teaching, especially during my student teaching semester, was that we had to keep our guard up and be on the safe side, so I limited the conversations and interactions in my classroom.

> Great teachers empathize with kids, respect them,
> and believe that each one has something special
> that can be built upon.
>
> —Ann Lieberman

My first year as a full-time teacher seemed to be going okay, but then things started to change. A few of the classes tried my patience. They questioned my methods, challenged me at times, and sometimes pushed back a lot. We had some rough patches; there were things that I could not seem to get a good handle on that led to my being placed on a teacher improvement plan. It completely shook my confidence, at least the little confidence that I had. The notification of my need for improvement came the day right before the holiday break, which gave me time to think about how to improve, but it also left me feeling scared of losing my job. Throughout the whole winter break I was worried, depressed even, afraid to return to school in January.

I realized there were issues in a few of my classes, but I didn't see them as major problems with my classroom management. The behaviors weren't bad; typically they came down to students making random noises or whistling occasionally while working, being off task, or disrupting one another by talking across the room. In my mind I had an excuse. My methodology courses did not provide me with a solid foundation, and I don't remember learning a lot of classroom management strategies. My experiences as a student teacher and a substitute did not prepare me for dealing with these behaviors because I had no issues during either of those experiences. As a student teacher, I taught in a classroom where students were active and did some cross-room talking, and sometimes hummed, but my cooperating teacher never addressed or redirected their behaviors. A semester of being in that kind of classroom helped to form my tolerance level for behaviors in my own classroom.

Trying to Find My Way

When I started the improvement plan, I felt so much stress every day. Some nights I had a hard time falling asleep because I worried what the next day would bring. Would I make the right choices? Would I be observed? Could I improve? I was constantly questioning myself, second-guessing most decisions, and isolating myself because I was embarrassed.

It weighed on me so much that when I would see my mentor, I instinctively expected to hear something bad. Always anticipating the worst, I avoided passing her room some days because I was afraid there would be negative feedback. I couldn't escape from feeling like I wasn't going to make it. Full of worry that I was going to make a mistake and that things would not get better, I chose isolation. It was an avoidance mechanism, as though hiding somehow would make my problems go away. It felt like I couldn't be me and that I had to be somebody different or else I would risk losing my job. I mostly avoided having conversations with students, and I felt as though I had to change my personality. On some days I didn't even know who I really was anymore. I was a young teacher trying to fit in, hoping to create a unique and fun learning experience for students while balancing the schedule and responsibilities of a first-year teacher. I often wondered if anyone else felt like I did, but I never asked because that meant sharing my struggles and what I considered to be failures. So I stayed in isolation.

*WHETHER YOU THINK
YOU CAN OR CAN'T,
YOU ARE RIGHT.
HENRY FORD*

Part of my teacher improvement plan required that I observe several teachers and write reflections on what I had observed, make comparisons with my methods, and set goals for the next steps of my plan. I used my planning period and sometimes lunch to do observations, and focused closely on the different teacher-student interactions within each classroom. I was curious about how some of my students acted in other classroom environments. Doing these observations helped me start to feel like I could make some changes and become a better teacher. I knew that what worked for someone else would not necessarily work for me, but I didn't have any other ideas to try, and so this is how I started.

What I noticed first was classroom management and that there were not any disruptive behaviors or issues similar to what I had experienced. The teachers that I observed had authority, but there was also a clear connection between them and the students. There were conversations as they welcomed students and interacted with each of them before class. I heard the teachers asking about sports, work, school, and life in general. Those interactions showed me the importance of learning about the students and letting them know that beyond the content, teachers are interested in who they are. It gave me a good reference point to better understand how to work on developing these relationships in my classroom. I had my own ideas, but for a long time I was still feeling like I had failed. Each time my mentor would tell me that we needed to talk, I feared the feedback that would be coming. I expected the worst and anticipated yet another failure. It was so hard to break away from feeling like a failure myself.

Heather Lippert, Kindergarten teacher, Cedar Valley Community School, @msyoung114

My hands started to shake, holding the lesson plan. I was being watched; every word I said was being typed into a document and analyzed. Was I using best practices? Was I saying the right words? Was I responding to student behavior in a positive way? These questions were flooding my mind, and I was trying to teach. Maybe I just couldn't do this.

It wasn't my best observation. My brain was telling me that I wasn't going to show my best teaching. I was so focused on showing "good teacher moves" that my teaching fell short. I believed that maybe I couldn't do it . . . and it showed in my practice.

Show up every day (observation or not) knowing that your practice is solid. Take a deep breath and exhale the shaky fingers; don't worry about what you are showing. Believe in your practice even when you are feeling the pressure of an observation. Know you can, and you will.

●●●

Heather's story resonates with me so well, and I wish I'd had her advice years ago. So many times I recall feeling overwhelmed by my fear of failing. My nerves were over the top. I was new, afraid to make mistakes, and aware that I lacked certain skills that teachers needed to have. If I would not have isolated myself, or had been part of a PLN like I am today, I would have had more resources for how to improve and make a difference. But the opportunities for connecting did not exist then as they do today, and time to collaborate with other teachers and meet with a mentor was limited—and in my case, sometimes avoided. And honestly, part of me was embarrassed that I was having problems at all. I had never experienced challenges with classroom management or student behaviors in all of the years that I had worked as a substitute, and I didn't understand why I was having them after nearly five years in the classroom. I also did not know how to fix them.

I thought it would be easier having my own classroom and that everything would just kind of fall into place. But it didn't. Admitting this to myself was tough, but confiding in someone else that I was struggling, and being paired up with additional mentors, let others know that I was not doing so well. It exposed my vulnerabilities and impacted my self-confidence for a long time. Students knew that I was struggling because they saw me observing other teachers, and some students overheard conversations between teachers about me. While it might not seem odd for teachers to observe one another, it was not as common of a practice then. I'm sure that many of my colleagues were aware of my struggles, which left me ashamed and embarrassed about it. Having my own insecurities about my skills and knowing there were others aware of my situation had a big impact on my confidence.

For a long time after that first year, I felt the effects of that improvement plan. Even to this day, it's still in the (almost) back of my mind, and those nerves and insecurities resurface now and then. It was a very difficult time for me, when I felt helpless. I worried about every class every day, constantly questioning my actions, and I struggled with knowing if I was responding to students in the right way. Did I need to be a strict teacher? That was not who I was. Should I laugh with students? Some people said not to smile until the holiday break, to set a standard. I wondered if I should, or could I ease up some? How many off-topic conversations or student behaviors should I be willing to accept and tolerate? Or maybe more accurately, how many were acceptable and not considered disruptive or detrimental to the learning environment? I lost the ability to distinguish and over-applied rules, and my tolerance of anything other than complete compliance was low. I've often wondered how many other teachers have experienced this, and if they had anyone to confide in. If you are going through something similar, please reach out to your PLN or build one. I've been through it and while I don't have all the answers, I am always available to share my experience. One thing I am sure of is that we all need support. Reach out to someone, make the changes you need, but don't lose who you are in the process.

> The greatest mistake you can make in life is to be
> continually fearing you will make one.
>
> —Elbert Hubbard

Every day left me feeling rigid and less like myself. I feared that the next phone call or observation would lead to another improvement plan—or worse, the need to look for a new position. I felt so different, and I was not being myself. I did not smile too often, was afraid to laugh, and rarely let my guard down because I didn't feel like I could. I can't imagine being like that today, but back then I was so afraid of making a mistake that I took fewer risks and simply tried to survive.

> # KEEP YOUR HEAD UP,
> # EVEN WHEN
> # YOU'RE FED UP.
> ## ~ALICE MERTON

No matter the struggles, you have to keep your head up. It took years of reflecting, connecting, and telling myself that I could make it through. I learned this, but it took some time for me to push down the fear of failing. I did the best I could to make progress every day. I tried some of the strategies that I had observed, like greeting students at the door, having everything ready for class, planning for every minute, and making sure that I was actively moving around the room. I became better at observing and listening. I think sometimes I was so wrapped up in covering the content, passing out papers, or writing on the board that I forgot about what was most important: the students. I needed to be more aware of what they were doing in class and how they were interacting with one another. Two areas that I really needed to work on were classroom management and student interactions. And honestly, it is difficult even after all these years of teaching to be aware of everything that happens in the classroom. It's easy to miss seeing things or hearing something that students might say to one another; their actions happen so quickly sometimes. The way to do better is if we don't stay planted in the front of the classroom.

After a few trying and exhausting weeks, I started to notice things about my students. I knew by their facial expressions when they understood the material and when I needed to explain a bit more. I moved around while asking questions or when students worked at their seats so I could interact with them. The more I did this, I started to see not just the class of students but each individual student. I understood their learning preferences, figured out their personalities, and even picked up on some of their interesting habits. It took a few months until I saw positive changes and my worries decreased, but those worries never fully went away and are still there today. What helped me to snap out of the ongoing worry was making time for those interactions with the students.

As teachers, is our goal to have perfectly quiet, compliant, fully engaged students in the classroom, sometimes working together but learning only from the teacher and without peer interactions? With some of the students that I had, silence for the whole class would not happen. There was always a pencil tapping, hands drumming on a desk, or humming. Noise like this can be distracting, but sometimes students just do it, and it might even go unnoticed by others. But is it something that I should interrupt the whole class for, just to redirect that one student? I didn't think that I should, and I let some of those behaviors slip by early on, which led to an improvement plan. I still question whether I was really lacking in teaching skills. Was I inconsistent with my strategies or had I not been providing the right types of activities based on student needs? I can wonder, but it won't change that experience. Even though I was sure I would fail, I pushed through. My skills continue to evolve because I opened myself to feedback, and I opened myself to connecting with students.

- Robert Allen

@SteinbrinkLaura

Maureen Hayes, K–6 Humanities Supervisor, Lawrence Township Public Schools, @mhayes611

We have heard it many times before: the best growth we can hope to face in all aspects of our lives is found through experiencing our own failures. Look at any major discovery or accomplishment that has made an impact or affected society as a whole, and you will discover a story of failure before accomplishment. It's what we do with our failures, how we use them and the feedback taken from them, that leads to reaching an end goal.

It is our responsibility as educators to continually provide our students with meaningful feedback that they can use to move forward in their learning and bring them closer to meeting goals. It needs to be okay to fail in our classrooms.

As a former first-grade teacher, I had the job of supporting students through the struggles and reinforcing the "yet" on the road to literacy. From Carol Dweck, the idea of a "growth mindset" and the use of the word "yet" to signify learning as a process, accepting failures and challenges as part of the growth process. It was my goal and responsibility to provide feedback and scaffold instruction until my students' failures turned them into readers.

I've had several "epic fails" as a teacher and administrator. Sometimes it's difficult in the moment to step back and look at a setback as a chance for reflection and growth, but with each experience I have benefited from the opportunity to move forward.

●●●

Recognizing Success

I think learning should be fun. Maybe that was part of my weakness. There were days when it was hard not to laugh at some of the things the students did. I felt compelled to maintain a quiet classroom and stop all of the disruptive behaviors, whether minor or major, even though many of them did not bother me or seem to bother the class. In the observations that I did, other classrooms had noise and discussions that veered from the content material and did not seem to be a problem for those teachers. I guess we just have to know where the line is drawn.

Students were very vocal, and it was not specific to my class, but rather how they interacted with other teachers. I spent time learning about each student because I was trying new things and opening up our classroom to learning beyond our space. I tried to bring in changes, thinking creatively and taking some risks, based on their interests. It was a unique experience to interact with such a diverse group of students. I learned new things about the teenage years and school experiences every day.

THE **MOMENT** you're ready to **QUIT** is usually THE **MOMENT** right before a **MIRACLE** happens. **DON'T GIVE UP!**

@wterral ~ Unknown

But the improvement plan reminded me that I could not become too comfortable—there had to be structure and discipline. There were still days when I wanted to quit because I felt that I just could not make the changes I needed to.

There were a lot of laughs and also moments when I thought about giving up because it felt like I wasn't reaching them. Some days we struggled, and other days I struggled a lot. It's difficult when you are trying to establish yourself as a leader by creating your presence in your learning space and figuring out how best to work with the students, especially when you first start teaching or are a new teacher at a school. Some students will try your patience, while others don't even think about it, and there are days when you might just feel like you won't succeed.

There were many struggles during that first year, probably because I came in thinking that I would have control of the classroom and wouldn't have any discipline issues because I never did before. I went into a classroom that had been run in a different way for half of the year, and I had to work with that while building my own style. I tried to teach using similar methods my own teachers used, and I think I had just assumed that the students would listen, would be respectful and excited for learning. I was wrong.

Letting My Guard Down . . . a Little

It took time. I kept trying to find my way and do the best that I could. I tried to relax and give students more control in the classroom, be open to their ideas and accept their random, silly behaviors. I wanted to act more like myself, rather than trying to fit the mold of a "model teacher" based on research and best practices. I wanted learning to be fun but was afraid to not follow a lesson plan. There is so much pressure to cover the curriculum and provide a structured lesson, and sometimes I think we just need to be ourselves, be flexible in our instruction, and take some risks. Be authentic with students and see what happens. If they suggest a different activity, then try it.

The first time I veered from the traditional lesson and gave students the lead was in a lesson about food with my Spanish III class. Students asked if they could prepare food from Spanish-speaking countries and have a party. Even the suggestion of a "party" made me nervous, so I made it clear that it was a learning experience, not a party. We would split class time between eating and learning activities. The students pushed back. It was not disrespectful, but they wondered why it couldn't just be time to interact and eat without any "learning." Why did we have to *learn*? Even though I thought that everything had to be scripted and all class time accounted for, I took a chance and tried it anyway. My hesitation was because my fear of making mistakes did not go away.

Fortunately it went well. But leading up to that day, their reference to a "party" and talking about it made me nervous. What if it was a disaster? What if we made a mess and behaviors were not good? What if I got in trouble for spending the class period focused more on eating rather than teaching? I worried a lot, but it worked out. I let my guard down a little and it was worth it.

A few times that year they brought in food prepared using recipes from Spanish-speaking countries, and we enjoyed the meal and time together. There was nothing like eating enchiladas at 9:00 a.m. or trying creations that looked less than appealing. It gave us time to bond, to relax, and to learn more about each other and other cultures. I started to realize that learning occurs even when it does not involve a worksheet or a defined class activity. I thought I had to provide something tangible for learning to actually occur, and based on something that I taught.

I learned a lot about my students and myself that year. Looking back leads me to reflect on where I started and serves as a reminder to myself that I had not failed. We have to take every moment we can to learn about our students and continue to push ourselves to become better. In doing this, we are better for them.

Questions for Reflection

1. Think about a time you experienced failure. What helped you push through and keep reaching toward your goal and finding success?
2. What are some strategies for encouraging students to break away from the instinctive "I don't know" response?
3. What can you do to worry less about making a mistake and focus more on trying new things? Where did you learn how to respond to failure?
4. What if: When was a time that you talked yourself out of trying something because of a fear of failing? Would you go forward with it now?

Share it out to #FUTURE4EDU.

Part II

BUILDING THE STRENGTH OF OTHERS

Chapter 7

LESSONS FOR LEARNERS AND LEADERS

School is so different now. I'm sure that many teachers who have been in the profession for ten, twenty, or more years would agree that the skills needed by educators today are unlike the skills needed in the past, and are very different from what most teacher preparation programs prepared them for. Educators were prepared to know the content, handle classroom management, and keep up with clerical responsibilities. Students also had to know the content, behave in class, and keep up with their homework responsibilities. But today, the skills that learners need the most are the ability to foster relationships in the classroom, strategies to develop social-emotional learning skills, knowledge of different learner needs, technology skills, training for emergency situations, and a keen awareness of and connection to peers. Educators' most important task is creating a space where all students feel safe, supported, and welcome. We must design a learning community full of choice and opportunities where all learners can thrive.

Getting to the Why

During my senior year of high school, I had no idea what I wanted to do after graduation. I was thankful that I had at least four years to figure it out while I was in college. In high school, I enrolled in the college-prep track, which was the only option because my parents had instilled in me that after high school I would go to college. Back then, there was an expectation that college was part of your life path. Not going to college was not an option for me, and I think many of my friends were in my same situation. In my high school, students were divided into different "tracks": college prep, business, or vo-tech.

As I think about it now, it seems strange to separate students like that: defining students based on the programs they were enrolled in. I wonder if some students in the college-prep program, including (but hopefully not) myself, looked down upon students who weren't in "our" program. Did teachers have lower expectations for the non-college-prep students? As students, we were made very well aware of each program and its requirements and goals, and it was clear which students were in the college-prep program.

Typically, college-prep students were thought of as students who worked the hardest, enjoyed studying, and would attend college and find good jobs upon graduation. Students in the business and vo-tech tracks would go straight into the workforce or possibly attend trade school after high school. Maybe they would own businesses someday, but a four-year college degree would not be part of their resumes, and at that time, that was kind of a big deal. Things have changed so much since then. Think about some of your closest friends who attended college and some who did not. What difference has it made in their lives? Are they doing what they thought they would be, or have they gone in a completely different direction? And think about classmates who were in your same track; did they go to college or in another direction?

The Skills All Students Need

Remembering some of the college prep courses that we had to take, I feel like we were not prepared for what college or life would require of us. We didn't have to take typing, learn shorthand, or do anything with personal finances, like learn to balance a checkbook. I don't know why these important skills were not part of our curriculum. I never learned the proper way to type, which made typing reports in college a bit of a struggle. To this day I don't really know how to balance a checkbook, don't even have one, and I am not too great with finances or creating spreadsheets. These might seem like small details now, but thinking back to high school, those are just some of the courses that I think we should have had the choice to enroll in, rather than having decisions made for us about what was important for our lives. Even consumer science courses, where students learned about responsibilities for maintaining a household, providing child care, and other life skills that everyone needs were not part of *our* curriculum. Apparently these skills were not necessary for us to be successful in life, but the college-prep courses like calculus and physics were.

I wonder how many schools might still be functioning like this today. Are schools designing curriculum and creating courses based on a system of tracking, or focus on college preparation, where students do not get to choose courses, but instead the choice is made for them based on test scores or some other type of standardization, rather than student interests? Do students have options to take a course based solely on their curiosity, rather than only choosing courses that will look good on a transcript for collegiate-level education? Do students get the chance to take courses they want, even if counselors or teachers think they might be too challenging for them? I don't want students being told that they cannot try something. We all need experiences and exposure to new ideas and possibilities. Who we are today does not determine who we can become in the future.

Often the [labels] kids receive become the LIES they believe. —Scott Kaufmann Hippert

The Importance of Connecting:
Social-Emotional Learning

In high school and even college, I wouldn't say that I fit into any specific clique or kept to only one group of friends. Not then and not now. As a kid, I was often excluded, including during classes when teachers chose team captains and let students create the teams. I was usually picked last. I really hated that practice. It felt awful being the only kid left standing there, not picked, until finally told by the teacher to join a team, a team who likely didn't want you anyway because they did not pick you. I remember trying to wave at my friends, who were already chosen, to vouch for me so the captain would pick me. It rarely worked, because I wasn't the fastest, the most athletic, or the most popular. I think that was a terrible practice that impacted student confidence, and is one of the main reasons that I prefer not to have students pick partners openly like that in my classroom. Exclusion hurts, and I never want students to feel like they don't belong and don't matter. Students need opportunities to work with people who are different than them. In those years of elementary school, it felt like I didn't belong. I wanted to be in a group, but I wasn't.

Even though I was not "in" one specific group, I enjoyed making connections with classmates from different tracks and groups. Graduating high school with a class of nearly six hundred, I knew most of my classmates by name and face to say hi, but I only got a chance to develop close connections and relationships with the classmates whose names were alphabetically close to mine and who were also college-prep kids. In homeroom the tracks were mixed, but when the bell rang, everyone went off within their own tracks for the rest of the day, except for lunch, if we were lucky to have different groups to sit with. Being separated like that did not help us to build social-emotional learning skills or to learn about our peers who came from different backgrounds and experiences.

> What you do makes a difference, and you have to decide
> what kind of a difference you want to make.
>
> —Jane Goodall

Kindness Matters

I've often wondered how I treated people in high school. I'd like to think it was with kindness and humor and without judgment. As a high school teenage girl, I'm sure that there was drama throughout those years, even though I cannot recall too much. I tried to stay away from getting in the middle of any problems between friends, and learned to think before I spoke to avoid saying anything hurtful. Words left a mark, and I learned from my parents to be kind, even when others are not kind to you. It matters.

I had experiences of being the one left out, or the one everybody was talking about—a friend one day and the person excluded the next. It hurt, and maybe that's why I feel so strongly about being an advocate for students, not only the ones in my class. I make it my goal to be aware of the interactions that go on in the classroom and to listen closely, be observant to make sure that students are treating one another with kindness and respect. Relationships are fundamental for learning to happen. All students deserve to feel like they belong because all students belong. Model kindness.

Maybe I'm more keenly aware of this today because of my own experience, and I recognize some interactions between students that remind me of what I went through. I pick up on the good, the bad, and the questionable. While many interactions are positive, there are just as many, if not more, that are negative, at least in my perception. Students say they are "joking with one another" because they are "friends," but I try to make the point that sometimes people won't admit when something is hurtful to them. Admitting that it bothers you makes you vulnerable, and for some, that is more uncomfortable than dealing with the comments or jokes. Students are often amazed at how much teachers see and hear while involved in doing many other things in the classroom. But that's what we have to do.

In my own experience, more often than not I accepted what others might have said to me rather than speaking up or trying to push back. Part of me wishes that I had had someone to step in during those times, and that is what pushes me to be different. Ask yourself what kind of person you needed when you were in school, whether a teacher you wish you had or a family member or other adult that you could have turned to, if you didn't have someone. As an adult, I strive to help students understand the importance of being kind and accepting others' differences. While not everyone will be your friend, nor will you be friends with everyone, it is important to treat others with respect, like they matter. We all matter. I recommend reading the book *A Passion for Kindness* by Tamara Letter, which is full of beautiful ideas for acts of kindness and will leave you inspired to do more and provide many ideas for you to implement with your students.

Gladiating for Our Students

Teachers are more than just the content deliverers. We are mentors, encouragers, coaches, even parental figures, and more besides the role of a classroom teacher. We have the power and opportunity to help students better understand each other and to be aware of the differences between us. It's in our control to create opportunities for students to work together and to build relationships, even if they are not friendships; it's the idea of being able to collaborate in the same space for the benefit of learning and growing. Everyone has something to offer, and we need to make sure that everyone is equally involved and feels important. Students need to know that they are supported, and sometimes that means we come up with a system to check on them or create a way for them to let us know when they need help. Sometimes that means trusting our students to take a step out of the classroom if they need to. But we won't ever know this if we don't take that time to engage in conversations and get to know them and build relationships. It always comes down to the relationships. The connections we make matter, more than we might sometimes even realize.

> Many of life's failures are people who did not realize how close they were to success when they gave up.
>
> —Thomas A. Edison

Failing just means that we need to keep learning. We need to create opportunities for students to explore and try new things, helping them to crush their own fear of failing. We may never realize which learning opportunities will lead students toward their futures, but we have to help open doors and maybe guide them to explore in a certain direction to get them started. We should not tell them where to look, but rather be available, observant, supportive, and ready to help if they need it, but also step aside quickly and let them carve their own ways in their own time. We must encourage them to try. Even when they push back, when they express that they don't think that they can do it, that they don't know how, we keep on encouraging. We have to show them that we want them to succeed by sharing that we too have struggled, and that anything worth having means that sometimes we have to accept defeat to find our path toward success. Remember that it's about the progress and growth along the way—the process. We can't back down because we tell ourselves that we can't do something. We won't know until we try.

> You don't have to be great to start,
> but you have to start to be great.
>
> —Zig Ziglar

Karyn Dobda, Educator, Pittsburgh, Pennsylvania, @kdobs1129
Each student who enters your classroom has unique skills, talents, and abilities that we must help him or her to discover. Helping

students to develop a growth mindset and believe in themselves is one of the most important things we can do for our students. "You never know what you can do until you try" is important for students to hear. Think about the last time you started something new. Remember how you felt? Anxious? Excited? Were you surprised by what you could accomplish once you took that first step? What did you learn about yourself? It is our responsibility as educators to help all students grow, develop, and achieve at the highest level of their abilities. All of our students have the ability to be great. It is vitally important that we create an environment that supports and nurtures them to take that first step, the first step on a path toward greatness.

•••

We Are Masters at Learning

We are all good at something, but we can't be good at everything, even if others expect that we should be. There are many times when people have asked me for help and I didn't have the answers. It was awkward saying "I don't know" or "I'm not sure." The responses I get are usually something like, "But I thought you knew everything?" I definitely do not.

Has this happened to you? If so, how did it make you feel? Because I work with technology a lot, I am often asked by students and colleagues to help with tech questions. Sometimes I find the problem quickly, which leads to a remark like, "Of course it's easy for you." Yes, but only because I put in the time. And sometimes I put in a lot of time and have felt helpless as I tried to find answers or master a new skill, occasionally even shutting down completely, nearly giving up because I just could not work through it and did not know where to turn for help. I don't always know the answers to the questions, but I do my best. Nobody sees the behind-the-scenes struggles that we went through in order to develop the skills which we seem so adept at. We either hide our struggles well or have not shared them with anyone, although we should. Showing our vulnerabilities and that we are still learning helps others to know that they are not alone in their own struggles. Nobody can know everything, but together we can keep learning more.

How Do We Learn?

A man should never be ashamed to own he has been in the wrong, which is but saying . . . that he is wiser today than he was yesterday.

—Alexander Pope

Throughout my life, from childhood until now, I have always been afraid of making mistakes. I don't know where this fear comes from, but it somehow seems to develop on its own, starting early in my life and continuing the older and wiser I get. It's rooted in self-doubt and reinforced by a lack of confidence in oneself, and it can manifest in different ways for different people. Sometimes this fear of making mistakes might cause you to completely shut down and give up something that you had already started. Other times it might stop you from taking a chance on something, whether it's a big or little risk. The fear of making a mistake leads to the decision to not even try it at all. Many times we may not verbalize our fears, but they show through our inaction. For others, the fear of making a mistake might manifest by saying things like "I'm probably wrong," "this probably isn't right," or "I don't know." Fear causes us to shut down, to back away from things that are challenging or scary. We can't let it. We need to think about fear differently, and in the words of Zig Ziglar, we need to think of FEAR as "Face Everything And Rise," rather than "Forget Everything And Run," regardless of how much we may want to at times.

Recognizing Fear

I don't know that I really recognized this verbalization of fear in myself until I started to see it in my students. When I would call on them in class, they would respond either that they couldn't answer or didn't know the answer. Sometimes I let them get away with saying "I don't know" and called on someone else. Why? I did it to help them avoid the embarrassment of being wrong in front of the class, partially because I could read their expressions and knew they were afraid to answer, and partially because it reminded me of my own weaknesses, especially with self-confidence and remembering how I felt in class when I didn't know an answer. I hoped to save them from that same feeling. But that is not how to help students become comfortable with mistakes and making growth. Now I don't accept those "I don't know" responses and instead encourage them to give the answer they had, and if it is wrong then that's okay because they are learning. We are all learning.

It makes me wonder if this fear of making mistakes is something that develops because of our learning experiences as children. Perhaps when we are corrected as children, because of behaviors or possibly in the classroom when we make a mistake, we develop this fear that becomes a bigger burden on us as time moves forward. Everybody wants to be right at least some of the time. Making mistakes might make you feel inferior, weak, inadequate, and probably even embarrassed. I have made a ton of mistakes; fortunately, some of the big ones have been when I was surrounded by only a small group, and many of those times were with friends and colleagues. I still didn't like the idea of making mistakes, but being surrounded by people who supported me and whom I felt comfortable with made a difference. It is great having a network to support you and say it's okay to embrace your mistakes. Of course, there are times when a person might call you out on your mistake and make you feel even more uncomfortable rather than trying to help you, build you up, and encourage you to move forward. If we want our students to take risks with learning and be okay with making mistakes, then we have to do the same and share our mistakes, especially while the students are there with us. Knowing that the fear of making mistakes and of not knowing an answer are common among my students, I am intentional about embracing and celebrating my own mistakes with them.

Sometimes we set ourselves up for failure. Fear of trying and failing, that mental process that happens when we listen to the inner voice telling us that we can't, leads us to believe it to be true. This phenomenon, referred to as "proactive paranoia," is something that I learned more about while reading *Escaping the School Leader's Dunk Tank* by Rick Jetter and Rebecca Coda. Jetter and Coda define it as the "anticipation of problems, negative reactions or responses of others"—a "healthy" type of paranoia that helps us to "get ready for battle."[1] I have done battle with that little voice inside of my head for years. Sometimes I cannot quiet the voice. A little voice that can do so much damage so quickly, fed by insecurities, self-doubt, and the need to protect oneself. The more often we tell ourselves something, whether true or not, the more we start to believe it. Convincing ourselves that we can't, before we even try, is no way to live and grow. Instead, we have to find a way to quiet that voice. By modeling this for students and then celebrating both failures and successes, we can encourage students to speak up, take chances with learning, and not be so afraid of making mistakes.

Where does that fear come from? How can we learn to quiet that voice, to become confident, and to help students rise above their fears and self-doubts? And how do we know if a student truly does not know, wants to avoid possible embarrassment, or has another reason for avoiding the question? It happens each day, in each class: students are called on and they respond with "I don't know" or statements of self-proclaimed doubt. It has become even more common this year, and I finally broke myself of the practice of letting

1   Coda, R., & Jetter, R. (2016). *Escaping the School Leader's Dunk Tank: How to prevail when others want to see you drown.* San Diego, CA: Dave Burgess Consulting.

students get out of responding when they say they don't know. I have noticed that saying "I don't know" often stems from a fear of being wrong or saying the wrong thing. Even as an adult, I have noticed there were times when I said "I don't know," sometimes because I truly didn't have an answer, or because the question was too complex and I was afraid to be wrong. Recognizing this in myself enables me to work harder to encourage students to respond.

When we use our own mistakes as a teachable moment to reinforce that it's more than okay to make mistakes, and guide students to respond confidently whether they are right or wrong, it is a step in the right direction. Students and even teachers can lose confidence quickly, which can lead to giving up, but when we send the message that others are likely to make the same mistake, too, we make progress. We're here to learn and grow together. It seems like an easy enough strategy and process, but even with consistent and intentional practice, it is still advice that I find difficult to follow.

We can be so critical of ourselves, and while to some extent we need to be when it comes to reflecting on our work, we also have to be self-aware. Being self-aware means recognizing our strengths and identifying areas we need to work on, and then using this information to help others to become better. We never stop learning, and there is always room to grow.

Perfect Does Not Exist

Nobody and nothing is perfect. Mistakes are everywhere—tiny flaws, minor and sometimes major imperfections. Our mistakes might impact only us, but sometimes we make mistakes that impact others. Even though how we handle mistakes makes a difference, we should still use them as a point of reflection, as a marker to pause and think about what we could have done differently. How do we react to our mistakes? If our mistakes impact others, we need to own this and make it our mission to be better every day after. We need to think about sharing our mistakes and our stories, because I truly believe that every person's failure is the key to somebody else's success.

What Does This Mean for Our Students and Our Colleagues?

Experience is simply the name we give our mistakes.

—Oscar Wilde

Have you ever felt like you are held to a higher standard, but feel like you don't meet it? Whether it's among friends or family, your colleagues, or even with members of your PLN and educational communities you belong to, you may have experienced the "imposter syndrome."[2] You develop a feeling that you aren't what you seem. Others have a certain belief about you and your abilities, or may think you have an area of expertise or skill that gives you an edge over others. Perhaps you did something to achieve this "status," but you may not believe it or see it in yourself. Knowing this perception of you exists can lead you to feel inferior and afraid of making mistakes if you don't live up to the expectations of others.

I have felt this "imposter syndrome" a lot. Whenever someone references me as having a skill or suggests that I know "everything," I feel my wall start to go up. Even hearing someone refer to me as being an expert makes me want to go back into isolation because of the fear of being wrong. Because I've always been really active with technology, I am often called, emailed, and visited by students and teachers who have questions about technology or digital tools to use. I've been asked to connect computers and to troubleshoot a lot of issues, and sometimes I know what to do, either because I learned it

---

2   Sindhumathi Revuluri, "How to Overcome Impostor Syndrome," ChronicleVitae, October 4, 2018, https://chroniclevitae.com/news/2112-how-to-overcome-impostor-syndrome?cid=VTEVPMSED1.

somewhere along the way or I had to learn it quickly on my own. Sometimes even just hitting a lot of buttons, doing a lot of right-clicks, and crossing my fingers, it somehow works out. But honestly, a lot of the time I don't necessarily know what to do. Being thought of as a "technology guru" brings a lot of pressure. I have felt like I won't be able to live up to some standard, and then feel like I'm letting someone down. To break free from this "imposter syndrome" we have to accept that while we may have some unique skill, qualification, or ability, we can't possibly know everything, and we are not perfect. We have to keep that in mind so that we don't talk ourselves out of a challenge or fear failures. Instead, we can avoid the imposter syndrome and just be who we are: mistake makers and courageous learners.

> If you're not making mistakes, then you're not doing anything. I'm positive that a doer makes mistakes.
>
> —John Wooden

Laura Steinbrink, District Communications Director and Webmaster, District Technology Integration Specialist, High School English Teacher, Plato, Missouri, @SteinbrinkLaura

I am constantly amazed by the number of educators who are uncomfortable, unwilling, anxious, or scared, or downright refuse to take a leap, try something new, or just push/click the button to see what happens. I don't know why this amazes me, but it does. Risk-taking is personal. It looks and feels different for everyone. I know that, but what I've also discovered is that what we each consider a "risk" varies considerably too. When a teacher puts me in front of his or her computer or device and explains the problem, generally I will ask if he or she has clicked here or pushed that, etc. The answer is usually, "I was afraid to do that in case I messed something up."

Okay, on one level I understand that. Nobody wants to be the one who breaks the school internet, but let's look at this in a broader sense. We create lesson experiences and activities for students, and then when one student stops at a certain point and won't progress due to fear of making a mistake, of messing things up, do we realize it's just like clicking this or pushing that button? Are we modeling risk-taking with our students? Once they see that we aren't afraid to try, to do it even though we might fail, and then try again, students will feel more confidence in pushing that button. So take a deep breath and let it out slowly. Now go ahead: push the button.

Every great story 📖
🌍 on the planet
happened when someone
decided not to give up,
but kept going no matter what.
-Spryte Loriano

Tisha Richmond

We have to be reflective each day and be okay with making mistakes because it will help us to become better for ourselves and our students. We must be mindful of our reactions to our own mistakes in the classroom because even when we don't think anybody's watching, our students are, and our reactions to setbacks are what can define us. We are role models for those we lead and learn with. We must show them that it is okay to fail and make mistakes; it's all part of learning and growing.

Don Sturm, Technology Integration Specialist, Former Social Studies Teacher, Morton Community School District #709, Morton, Illinois, @sturmdon

It is human nature to watch people who are experts at something and think to yourself, "Wow . . . they make that look so easy." This goes through my mind every time I watch an Olympic athlete perform or read a book by a prolific author. Becoming an expert at anything requires countless hours of dedication. In fact, some would estimate the time needed to gain true expertise at around ten thousand hours, though there is some debate about this number. No matter the true number, expertise is hard work, and it is important to understand and respect that fact. It is also easy to just assume that some people are better at things than others.

I see this daily in my job as a technology integration specialist. I will show a teacher something for which I have spent countless hours experimenting, failing, and trying again, and hear, "It must be nice to be that good with technology." A perfect example is using Google Sheets, which does not come naturally to me. I was trying to create a way for teachers to submit a Google Form evaluation for professional development that would, in turn, generate a PDF that they could use as evidence for their license renewal. It took a number of hours of reading, watching YouTube videos, designing, and testing to be able to perform this "easy" task. A few teachers commented that they wished they had the knowledge to use Google Sheets like this in their classrooms. But they were not present to see the amount of time and resources it took for me to develop that skill and comfort level. As educators, we cannot limit ourselves by comparing our skills with those of others, who may have invested many hours, experienced failures and even frustrations before mastering a certain skill. If we do, then thinking like this would lead educators to shy away from trying new things because they believe they will never be as good as they think they need to be. The only way to get better at anything is through practice.

QUESTIONS FOR REFLECTION

1. Think of a time in your life as a student when you felt left out or excluded. Was there someone there to support you and lift you up? How did it impact you?
2. What is a skill that you have, in which others may think of you as an expert, but is an area that was challenging for you? Did you feel like giving up but pushed through? Have you shared your story with anyone?
3. How can you help students to build their own supportive networks in the classroom?

Share it out to #FUTURE4EDU.

Chapter 8

UNDERSTANDING SCHOOL
AND LEARNING TODAY

I often wonder what the public's perception is of the educational system and life in schools today. There are so many changes happening: new initiatives, new types of schools, new strategies and tools, and new roles besides "teacher." There are also many challenges that go along with being in education that require ongoing training and professional learning. It is important that we share the story of school and what education looks like today and moving forward. But how?

We can start by involving our colleagues and communities in discussions about what school should look like and how to best provide for our students. By asking for feedback, we can get a mix of perspectives and backgrounds to design a plan to meet all needs and work together.

This could be a conversation with a mix of educators and non-educators, and current and former students of different educational backgrounds (based on location, type of school, class size, year of graduation, courses studied, and involvement in school activities). Participants could share their definitions of what school *should* look like, describe a classroom of today, and explain how they envision learning happens best.

There would no doubt be a wide variety of responses, some positive and others quite negative. Many of my non-educator friends have an idea of some of the changes in school, perhaps because they have children in school and are struggling with the changes in testing, the amount of homework, and the different structure for learning that exists compared to what they remember. Others have been out of school for a long time or do not have children currently in school, and their recollection may be a mix of what they remember from being a student and what they have heard from educators or through social media or news sources.

Teaching Is Easy, Right?

From the outside looking in, being a teacher may seem like quite a comfortable job: Monday through Friday, weekends off, school hours—and there's also that summer break. When it comes to trends in education, most might be familiar with things like Common Core, educating the whole child, standards-based grading, STEAM, and social-emotional learning, to name a few. But does being familiar with or having a basic understanding of these offer a clear picture of what all of that involves? Not really. There is so much more to teaching than there was five or ten, let alone twenty or more, years ago. It becomes more challenging each year, contrary to a longstanding belief that it becomes easier. A lot of the changes come down to the use of technology for facilitating different learning opportunities for students, the clerical tasks and training that teachers are responsible for, and new initiatives that teachers must balance in their already busy schedules. Besides the teaching and task-oriented responsibilities, there are times that may require us to push aside teaching the content and instead work with each student. Students come first.

Curriculum or Curiosities?

We have to look at school and learning differently today. Are we in the "business" of simply delivering content to the students and having them give the content back to us in projects or assessments, and then move to the next topic? Do we determine our instruction based on the "canned curriculum" of our textbooks, preparing students for the test, or what we have been doing for years, the "that's the way we've always done it" mentality? I admit that I was doing this, using the book as my guide, following only what it included and the curriculum that I had partially created based on it. I worried more about finishing the program and following the book's pace, rather than making adjustments based on student needs and interests. I am definitely not proud of this, but I was doing what I thought I needed to do the way that I had always done it. Teaching a new course always felt like such a challenge, and I lacked the confidence to design my own plan, so I followed what was in place and relied on my own experiences as a student. We can't rely on the methods and tools that we've been using or that worked for us. We have to go beyond that and explore new ideas that will push us to create something new and different and exciting for our students. What will keep us relevant? It's not enough for us to just know the content; we need to keep learning and let students explore on their own, or we run the risk of failing our students. We cannot limit them to the knowledge we have.

More Than the Content

Being in education today is challenging. Our roles have been redefined. We have a lot to balance just to stay current with best practices and new technologies. But we must also be ready to support the needs of our students and colleagues, not be afraid to stretch ourselves professionally, and in today's world be a source of unwavering strength and courage when the unimaginable or unthinkable happens. There are moments when we are called into action with little to no time to prepare. For this reason, we must always consider the what-ifs and be ready to create a path to lead the way and keep our students safe.

In *Culturize*, Jimmy Casas reminds us that leadership is "not just about how we behave when we know what to do . . . but seen in the action we take when we don't know what to do."[1] We need to not only immerse ourselves in professional learning but also be relentless in our pursuit of new opportunities for those we learn and lead with. We are servant leaders, placing others' needs before our own and fostering relationships built on trust, transparency, honesty, courage, and empathy. We walk with purpose and are clear on our why. We are dedicated to cultivating a network and a mindset for learning. To do so means we push ourselves to develop and model the skills and qualities that we want to instill in others. We lead but must learn first. As Casas says, "Our work is never done."

Our work requires us to continue building our knowledge and learn how to fail, reflect, and try again. Through self-awareness, grit, and reflection, we know that failure is not final, only a temporary challenge on the path to success. These are qualities and habits that we need to model for students and colleagues. One of the most important skills we need to develop is the ability to be self-aware. Being self-aware means you recognize strengths and weaknesses, emotions, and thoughts and have a deeper understanding of what motivates you. I often say that I am a work in progress, and with each passing day I become more self-aware of who I am as a professional and as a person.

There are specific areas that I need to devote extra time to in order to become more effective and consistent and maybe even achieve some balance in my life. I imagine that there are many educators who set high demands and feel like there is never enough time. Doing what is best for our students and ourselves without balance can lead to burnout and disengagement. We overextend, but our motives are clear: passion for learning and leading, persistence for growing, and rising above challenges.

---

1   Casas, J. (2017) *Culturize: Every student, every day, whatever it takes.* Pgs. 81 and 113. San Diego, CA: Dave Burgess Consulting.

Balance Is Hard to Find

We know the importance of balance but still overextend ourselves. "No" is one of the most difficult words for us because our work is never done. Personally, I have not felt as productive as I want or need to be. How do we achieve balance, when doing so means we may let others down or not fulfill personal goals? And more importantly, how can we keep focus when surrounded by and consumed by constant "connectedness?" We rely on our PLN to help us learn, grow, find balance, and even share frustrations. Without a supportive network, breaking away from the isolation that can happen is more difficult. Our answer to finding balance and being the best version of ourselves is to be surrounded by people who will push and challenge us. Together we can achieve more and do more for those we lead.

We Are in Competition Only with Ourselves

Do you see educators who put themselves out there, teaching, writing, and traveling, who somehow maintain balance, the balance that you dream of but just cannot find? How can we keep up? Even routines sometimes are short-lived or lack consistency often because we add more to our responsibilities and time commitments. Some days I just can't keep up with life in general. I feel frustration at falling behind, letting others down, and not pushing myself enough to accomplish more. And more times than I want to admit, I get completely overwhelmed to the point that I want to give up. Do you wonder how many other educators struggle or doubt their abilities and even feel inadequate?

I wondered, but I did not ask. It's the fear of showing vulnerability. Instead, I took time to read books that I thought might push my thinking about school and how to do better for students. I chose *The Path to Serendipity* by Allyson Apsey and *What School Could Be* by Ted Dintersmith. Reading these books gave me clarity and hope. I recognized that the very thing I try to stop my students from doing is what I do: push myself so hard, judge myself so critically, and doubt my abilities, to the point where my desire to work becomes consumed. I feel myself freeze, put up a wall, and cannot quiet that inner voice telling me that I will fail. That voice often wins.

Be the Strength for Others

Students push themselves so much, filled with worry they won't be as smart as their peers, won't get into college, won't get the highest grade. It saddens me to see doubts at their young age, and that feeling of not meeting some "standard." My own struggles with feeling inadequate drive me to lift them up. I tell them, "You don't need to worry about anybody else. You only need to worry about you and what is best for you." I share a quote that I remind myself of often: "I'm in competition with no one but myself." How can I be better for them when some days I struggle with the same thing?

Be Brave and Dare Greatly

A good friend of mine, Mandy Froehlich, wrote *The Fire Within*, a book full of personal and educator stories that share adversities experienced. We don't often hear others' stories, especially of adverse experiences, but we need to. When we start with relationships, open and vulnerable, we continue to learn and grow. Sharing stories of epic failures, times of disengagement, or great successes helps us realize we are not alone. While telling our stories makes us vulnerable, tremendous power lies in vulnerability. In *Daring Greatly*, Brené Brown said vulnerability is "the courage to show up and be seen even when you have no control over the outcome." I remind myself of this quote when my insecurities or fears start to win over. When I think back to the improvement plan from more than twenty years ago, and that fear creeps in again, I remember that it is better to try and fail than to never have tried at all. The title, *Daring Greatly*, was inspired by a speech given by Teddy Roosevelt in 1910. In Roosevelt's speech, he spoke about the man who enters into battle valiantly, and at best he succeeds and at worst he errs while daring greatly. The lesson is that we must try, try again and not give up. Try and fail, maybe, but rise and try again. Even when you feel like you can't.

> There is no innovation and creativity
> without failure. Period.
>
> —Brené Brown

Failures and Moonshots:
No Success Without Failures First

Moonshots. The world is amazing. Think about inventions, chances, and "moonshots" taken by leaders, educators, explorers, inventors, scientists, athletes—anyone really. How long did it take for success to happen? Just look at the different technologies we have today, and think about all of the iterations, failures, and near wins that were part of the experience. Still, technologies are not perfect; there are always going to be mistakes. And how do we define "success"? Is it simply the absence of failure?

There are mistakes in everything. Listen to famous speeches, presentations, TV programs, or radio talks: mistakes are made often. Musicians play notes wrong, dancers miss steps, athletes miss points or have off days with skills, publishers and authors miss typos in books. Mistakes are everywhere. Even teachers make mistakes with content they are teaching. Everyone makes mistakes. It's what we do with them that makes the difference. But we can forget this when we see somebody who looks successful, has achieved some great recognition, or created something. You might not realize what it took to get there. To throw out a few examples, look at Thomas Edison, Michael Jordan, J. K. Rowling, and Arianna Huffington.

More Than 20,000 Failures with Four Great Successes

We know why Thomas Edison became famous: inventing the light bulb and holding more than 1,000 patents. Did you know it took him nearly 11,000 tries to figure out the light bulb? We look at the end product and think, "Wow, that's genius. How did he do that?" We don't often think about all of the time it took to finally have success. Imagine if he gave up. Would someone else have created the light bulb by building upon his failures? Or would we be in the dark? And how about athletes? Take Michael Jordan. It is said that he missed 9,000 shots in over 300 games, and when he had an opportunity to win the game in the final shot, he missed twenty-six of those shots. Failures? Yes, but people don't look at all of the statistics; they see the accomplishment and success. The high point of his career becomes a standard of comparison, which most everyone will be unable to match. Jordan said, "I've failed over and over . . . and that is why I succeed."

Look at J. K. Rowling, turned down by twelve different publishers, who then ultimately achieved tremendous success with her Harry Potter books. Her message was that she wished someone had taught her how to handle failure, that failure is inevitable but it's what you do with it that makes a difference. Arianna Huffington, author of thirteen books and president and editor in chief of the Huffington Post Media Group, experienced failure when her second book was rejected by thirty-six publishers. She said, "Failure is often the key to success. You can recognize very often that, out of these projects that may not have succeeded themselves, other successes are built." I believe this is key.

If we think about these four people and other similar stories of success and failure, we can imagine how different the world might be had they given up. Things we use in our daily lives might not even exist if these people and others like them gave up after the first failure. There are different definitions and levels of success, and we don't need to match the success of others; we need only to create our own path to success. Our path is created by making mistakes along the way and taking what we learn, building upon it, and becoming even better.

Mistakes Happen a Lot

In reading this book, I guarantee you will find mistakes, whether a word that is out of place or missing, incorrect punctuation, a grammatical structure that just does not seem to flow, or a thought that trails off. No matter how many times it gets reviewed before it's published, how often I have read it through, mistakes will be missed. We can fix these mistakes, and most times we can determine what the author intended. While mistakes might be distracting when you notice them, please let me know when you find one. This is how we help ourselves and others to improve. During law school, I remember finding so many errors in the big law books. Some were minor and didn't impact my concentration too much, but some led me to completely lose my train of thought. I would lose my focus on the details of a court case or some rule of law. I had to reread the whole section to refocus. My close reading skills improved, and I realized that people make mistakes, and that being an author, or a publishing company, does not exclude you from making mistakes. However, my perception was that the books, the authors, and the publishing company would be perfect. But nothing is perfect, and that is okay.

Teach Content or Teach Students?

Are we simply teaching the content and then asking students to basically repeat the information back to us, maybe in a slightly alternate format? Do we use worksheets or other activities that simply require lower-level recall, with no opportunity for extended learning, creativity, or choice? If so, then we are not pushing student thinking high enough and preparing them for their future by having them minimally interacting with the content. We need to stretch our own thinking and create innovative and uncommon learning experiences for our students and for ourselves. To do this might mean that we ask students for ideas to help us think differently than we traditionally have. And we have to be okay with doing this. Education is changing and we have to change too. We need to lead the change.

Diverging from the Plan

Almost every day students ask to make a shift in the "plan." Sometimes they ask to play a game, or work with a partner, or have a study hall. Years ago

I was not okay with their suggestions, and I think I even reacted negatively at times. I had a lesson plan I intended to follow. But now I am okay with their ideas, which surprises me as much as it surprises them. I have a more flexible mindset, and students have even commented that I am "chill." (I think that is a good thing.) While not every idea works out well, I am often willing to give it a go. Why? Because the experience of learning needs to be different for every student, and decisions in the classroom should not be made only by the teacher. We should involve students because they are directly impacted by our actions. If we do not promote choices and help them to feel valued, then we are not providing all that we need to. Sometimes, though, we need to actually provide less, meaning that we should be flexible by not planning for every single class minute. Learning needs to be spontaneous.

@STEINBRINKLAURA

An important part of our mission is to engage all students in learning, and this cannot be done by giving every student the exact same thing. Are we interested in pushing compliance or in promoting choices and creating opportunities? Take a minute to think about your own professional development experiences and equate them with how students might feel about learning in your classroom and in school. What are your feelings about professional development sessions where everybody gets the exact same experience or training? Have you sat through something that did not directly apply to your practice? How engaged in the session were you? It's the same if we offer only one option for students. True engagement will not happen without relevance and meaningful learning experiences. Do we as educators have an opportunity to share ideas, suggest different activities, and voice our interests? Or do we simply have to comply? Aside from PD training sessions that we all need, we also need to design our own learning paths. And so do our students.

Throw the Plans Away

How awesome would it be to take time in your classes and, instead of having scripted plans in mind or activities made and ready to go, toss them aside and, on the spur of the moment, make something up. Seriously. We've all had enough experience thinking quickly or coming up with a backup plan when something doesn't work as we hoped, and if not, then this is the chance to model risk-taking in the classroom. I have told students that sometimes I make it up as I go.

Pick a day to kind of go with the flow and be flexible with your instruction. Let students know that you don't really have a plan in mind, and you are counting on them for ideas, reminding them that it is a little bit of a risk, which you hope will work out. But if it doesn't, it's a good experience and lesson to share with students. Together you can think about why it didn't work and try again. It becomes a shared story to tell and reflect on as new challenges and opportunities to take risks present themselves. Encourage their "I wonders" and what-ifs.

Jon Craig, Instructional Coach, Harry S. Truman High School, Bristol Township School District, @coachjoncraig

Technology in the classroom can do many things. Provide a voice for students who may be physically unable or who struggle with anxiety. Be a translator for non-English-speaking members of our community. Knock down the walls of classrooms and instantly connect our students with classrooms and experts from all over the world. Technology can do great things, but replacing a great teacher is not one of them.

Google and YouTube have an overabundance of content, but they cannot, on their own, perform the many tasks performed by a great teacher on any given day. Building relationships; providing specific, actionable feedback; making adjustments to lessons in real time; and providing students with exactly what they need, when they need it, are a few tasks that make great teachers irreplaceable. When these tools become part of their practice, this combination of teaching practice and technology leads to authentic learning experiences that will inspire, empower, and motivate students to strive for greatness. We owe it to students to overcome our own apprehensions, fears, and hesitations when it comes to technology as we confidently embrace technology as a means to support us, not to replace us.

●●●

Technology will change, but one thing that will be a constant is the importance of teacher-student relationships in the classroom. We need to focus our efforts on fostering these connections, and then everything else can fall into place when we have that solid foundation. We have to be okay with taking risks and diving in, knowing that we might not have all the answers, that we might fall flat on our faces, but also that we have the skills to push through and use those mistakes as a learning experience. When we create these solid foundations and nurture relationship-building and risk-taking in the classroom, we help students build skills and become confident to venture bravely out on their own.

Questions for Reflection

1. Think about some recent lessons that you taught. Did you follow a plan or allow for spontaneity in learning? How could you have?

2. Think of one lesson that you taught in which you lectured or led all of the activities. Now think of a way to give students the lead.

3. What is one change you want to make based on something you read in this chapter?

Share it out!

Choose a quote from this chapter and share your story to

#FUTURE4EDU.

Chapter 9

EMPOWERING STUDENTS BY STEPPING ASIDE

The greatest sign of success for a teacher is to be able to say, the children are now working as if I did not exist. Maria Montessori

@woodard_julie

How often do you catch yourself answering questions in class? My students ask a lot, and many times I find myself answering the same question for multiple students. It became a habit. They asked and I answered. It did not seem like something that I shouldn't do, until I realized that by answering their questions, I was taking away their opportunity to think, struggle, and exceed my own knowledge. I was removing a chance for them to learn.

Knowing this, I try to resist the urge to answer right away or even give a hint. These are some of the habits we may have as teachers, and some that we need to break in order to help our students thrive. We need to find ways to empower students to drive their learning and make choices based on *their* interests and needs. What do they want to learn? I've noticed a shift happening in instructional strategies based on research, data, and—perhaps what I hope to be part of the catalyst for—student voice. My hope is that students feel comfortable and confident advocating for themselves and sharing their ideas with a public audience beyond their teachers and classmates. We should be offering more authentic learning opportunities to connect with the content in meaningful ways and give students a choice in how to apply their learning. We can no longer have each student completing the exact same task. Students need to be able to find their own answers and come up with their own driving questions.

I believe that preparing for our classroom instruction today is less about teaching the class and more about teaching the student. Time spent should be focused on having students be active, doing more than consuming, by becoming creators. They need space to learn on their own and to experience productive struggle. It's more than just providing opportunities for students to explore; it's about getting out of their way so they have space to design their own learning paths.

It's Our Learning Space

For so long, classrooms have been teacher centered and teacher driven. All students complete the same or very similar tasks, with little opportunity if any to determine their own directions for learning. This was my classroom for years. Creating this type of freedom in the classroom is challenging, especially for teachers like myself who had been using traditional methods for a long time. But we can all change. It may not happen overnight, and it might not be without difficulties. It feels uncomfortable because it's unconventional. Any time we take a risk with something new, it's going to involve feelings of unease and uncertainty. But our position enables us to take those risks, and we should because of the potential for amplifying student learning.

Teachers have been the leaders and key decision makers in the classroom for years. But it's time to make some changes, to transform what classrooms look like, and welcome the struggles that are a part of it. They are not insurmountable challenges that we cannot work through, but rather short-term steps or hurdles to jump that are necessary for long-term success. When students have an opportunity to explore on their own, make the decisions, and learn in innovative ways, it becomes *their* classroom. Moving away from a one-size-fits-all assignment or activity to those that are hands-on and student-driven, learning becomes more meaningful and relevant for students. Meaningful learning experiences lead to higher student engagement and motivation.

Jere Brophy said that when we provide diverse, hands-on learning opportunities for students, it will lead to higher engagement when they have a sense of ownership that comes about by choice in learning. It will serve as a catalyst for fostering intrinsic motivation, and this is what we want. We want students to be intrinsically motivated to learn, to explore, to challenge themselves without focusing on grades, points, or incentives. We learn by doing.[1]

Daniel Pink said that motivation is based on autonomy, mastery and purpose. So the key is giving students the choice and opportunity (autonomy) to continue to grow and to feel challenged (mastery), and for it to be meaningful (purpose). Our goal is to be there to support students in their transitions and learn from them.

Beyond just having students create a project and choose from different formats to create, student choice and voice means letting students make these decisions. When we don't provide an end goal or template, we place emphasis

---

1   Brophy, Jere E. *Motivating Students to Learn*. 2nd ed. Mahwah, NJ: Lawrence Erlbaum Associates, 2004.

on the process of learning rather than the end product. The key is to instead empower the students to decide how to show what they know and not tell them to create some specific end product. This lets them choose to apply their learning in a way that is meaningful and personal to them. When students have autonomy, they become more engaged and the potential for learning increases. We must give them time to draw from their experiences, think about their interests, and collaborate with peers. We can help students develop their skills by encouraging them to establish their own learning communities in the classroom. Learning communities are the most beneficial when students feel comfortable, cared about, and empowered in their learning.

Empowering Students by Focusing on Learning, Not School

In 2015, I started to change some things in my classroom. I recall my frustration with a couple of different issues that I have referred to over the years as a "disconnect." A disconnect was when students who had been absent showed up in the middle of the class period and asked for help. It bothered me that they had fallen behind and that I could not give them the attention that they needed when they showed up. Other times, students would come to see me before or after school, but I was either in a meeting or had already left for the day. Typically I would find notes left on the board or my desk, but not until the next morning, so opportunities for learning were being lost. The student who had the question had to go without an answer, or the other students had to wait during class while I tried to help the student who showed up. I needed a way to be accessible, and for students to be able to find resources when they needed them.

In my mind, there was nothing worse than a student trying to do work at home at night or over a weekend and being stuck, unable to complete the work because of an absence or maybe because of just being zoned out in class. We know this happens, even to us as adults in meetings; sometimes we are not fully present. Next time you are in a meeting or a PD session, take a look around. How many of your colleagues are truly listening? And how many are involved in other things like checking email, browsing online, grading papers, or just talking? It amazes me that the behaviors we as educators wish to stop in our classrooms are the same ones that we engage in ourselves. When it comes to our students, we have to prepare for times when they miss out in class, and when they have the time to focus. Unfortunately, it might not coincide with when we are together in class.

When You Don't Know What You Are Looking For

Google it. Google comes in handy when you are looking for something but are not sure exactly what. Machine learning and artificial intelligence can populate resources from random search terms and make finding something that you didn't even realize you were looking for happen much faster. Or now, ask Alexa or Siri or any other virtual assistant.

I googled something like "website disconnect, app messaging," and there were millions of responses within .3 seconds. The first one that I recognized was Blackboard. Several teachers in my school were using it, but I took one look at it and decided that it didn't seem like something I could implement quickly enough to help my students. A few search results down, I clicked "Edmodo," and when I looked at it, I knew it was exactly what I was looking for. Students weren't thrilled at first because Edmodo was something different and they did not understand why I was using it. But after a little time, there was progress: a decrease in the number of students showing up in the middle of a class looking for help or papers, and students were using the resources available on Edmodo as a centralized place for us to connect.

Building on that, we started to use Celly, a messaging app. I wasn't really sure how it would work, but it was fun trying it with students and seeing our "disconnect" continue to disappear. Students started to advocate for themselves by using these tools to create new ways to communicate and learn. We had connected. It was working.

That One Student

I remember the start of my transition from doing the "job" of teaching. It was around nine forty-five on a Friday night when I received a question from one of my Spanish II students who was working on a project due the next day. My students knew they could ask questions at any time, but were reminded that if it was too late in the evening, my response would have to wait until the next morning.

The best thing about using these tools is that it creates more flexible learning time, learning that continues beyond the time and space of the classroom. Students can ask questions and submit work beyond the school day. I appreciated that this student was working on Spanish on a Friday night. The question was about which tool to use for the cartoon project. Students had time over a two-week period to work on the project in class. My practice is not to hover but to give them independence to work on their own. For this student, it had come down to the last twenty-four hours, and the pressure was on to get something done. I sent some ideas and answered a few questions, and sometime later that night, hours after I had already gone to sleep, an amazing project was created.

Realizing the Importance of Connecting

It was the moment I realized how important it is that we are available. The Spanish II cartoon project was so well done and creative. The student who created the project often worried a lot about grades and not doing well, as students will. There were doubts about language ability and also a lack in self-confidence that students struggle with as they transition through high school. A message included with the project said something to the effect of "This is probably terrible and all wrong," and it may have even been titled "My Awful Project," but it was far from it. I received several thank-yous and sorrys for being available to answer "so many questions" on a Friday night and for being so patient. It was an opportunity to be "present" when a student needed me beyond the school day, and an affirmation that having the right tools in place makes such a difference.

The project really was amazing. I remember it like it was yesterday and have used that project as a learning tool with other classes many times. It is way more authentic than showing a YouTube video or having students listen to me most of the time. It is the why behind setting up an access point for students to communicate when they need help, and a story that I have shared with others who question why I'm so willing to answer questions on a Friday night, early on a Sunday morning, or over a holiday break. Why wouldn't I? I am invested in helping students when they need help, which sometimes includes weekends or later in the evening. Rather than answer, I ask, "Why not?"

Being accessible to our students is what we are here to do. As educators, we are not in a "job" that ends when the bell rings, and it does not stop over the weekend. We are in a profession, responsible for educating others and dedicated to the lifelong pursuit of learning and growing. We must strive to provide the same thing for those we work with, which means that we need to be available to students when they need it, and that often means beyond the school day. Our responsibility to students does not end when they leave our classrooms. When a teacher begins to feel this way, it is time to make a change.

Being available for that student made a difference. Connecting and supporting her as she worked, and validating her efforts afterward, lifted her up and enabled me to see more clearly what students need and deserve from teachers: our time. There was worry about mistakes, but what mattered was that she created something authentic and meaningful and advocated for herself. Even though it came down to the last twenty-four hours before it was due, without that access in place, an opportunity for learning would have been lost. Being able to ask for help and get feedback beyond the limits of the school day makes a difference. It's how it should be. Beyond high school, whether in college or in work, we can access information and assistance when we need it, so why should it be different for students? Without this access, students lose out and may end up frustrated, whereas by having a way to connect as they work, they will be more confident and comfortable when advocating for themselves.

Lessons Learned

That Friday night was the push that I needed to really evaluate the work that I was having my students do and the importance of creating a connection with them. It led me to actively look for opportunities and showed me the value in setting up different ways to connect. My goal of being available for questions served an unexpected purpose: building relationships and redefining my definition of a teacher. It helped me to see the difference between assigning specific projects and giving students the power of choice. That single interaction was enough proof that I had taken a step in the right direction and motivated me to keep going. I knew that deciding to use a messaging app was making a difference, even though some people thought it was too much, that I didn't need to be available all the time. But that's not how I felt. And since most everything I believed about teaching had been wrong, and I had made a shift away from traditional methods anyway, I believed I was on the right path to becoming a better teacher. That Friday night message was the start of a connection with a student who became confident and creative and benefited from this way to connect. Even on vacation, messages would come asking for websites and readers online, because she had forgotten her materials and did not want to fall behind. This is a student I will always hold very dear to my heart. Looking back over those interactions, knowing that I was available when a student needed me, is when I developed and better understood my why.

Being Accessible Matters

Have you set up different ways for others to connect with you, besides traditional email? Email was not something that I considered, and when I initially started using Celly and Edmodo, it was out of the frustration that I was feeling, and that students were probably feeling too. My purpose was to decrease the number of times students came to class unprepared. I thought that taking time to set something up would create more time in the long run, time that would be better spent learning and building confidence rather than experiencing frustration and falling behind. It took a little time, but what I started to notice was that students were reaching out. Students who did not ask for help or were rather quiet in class started to develop their voices. Relationships were forming, students were leading, and things were improving.

Being accessible and providing students with choices in how to show learning is so important. In my experience, I became comfortable with doing less of the decision making and being open to student-driven learning. I learned about my students in a shorter period of time. Together we created new connections and a more positive classroom culture. The realization came that the "access points" served a greater purpose, not simply a solution to frustration any longer. Creating these access points showed students that they didn't just matter while in the classroom; they always mattered and could get support whenever they needed it. Technology makes it possible to guide students as they work through an assignment or a project beyond the school day. Learning doesn't stop. Beyond understanding their skills in the content, we can learn more about them and their interests. It is the start of looking for additional ways to share what students are doing. We need to find ways to empower them in the classroom, and this can evolve into empowering them out of the classroom as well.

Being Their Advocate Matters

What are the opportunities for students to share their work? Are there student showcase events or community nights to share the work being done in our schools? How about having students lead a tech night, inviting members of the school community in to learn some new tech ideas, explore some STEAM projects, and see what is going on in education today? There are lots of possibilities for doing this, and for us, the first was an educational technology conference, PETE&C (Pennsylvania Educational Technology Expo and Conference), held yearly in Hershey, PA. Part of the conference involves a student showcase, and after some success with changes I made, I decided to apply to take a group.

This was a big step. It was the first time I would be doing this and also putting myself out there because I applied to present a session of my own. As someone who did not like public speaking and avoided speaking in front of peers at faculty meetings, I couldn't believe that I actually clicked "submit" on the proposal. If accepted, I would be presenting to a room full of educators I did not know, and for some reason I was seemingly okay with that. I wonder if other educators have that same fear or get nervous when they have to speak in front of colleagues, even though they speak in front of students every day. To me there's just something different about speaking in front of one's peers. Knowing my struggles with self-doubt and lacking in confidence, I didn't think I would get accepted anyway. I had only just begun my learning journey with technology, and I knew there were many other more qualified people.

Applying to be a presenter was definitely a new experience and a risk, but one that I needed to take. When we ask our students to take similar risks, we should be prepared to do the same. What kinds of role models would we be if we didn't also take some risks and challenge ourselves?

Growing Together Matters

We were all accepted, and a group of ten students presented, setting themselves up behind tables and displaying their projects on their computers. They invited people over, asking them to try a game they created or look at their projects. I stood off to the side and observed, listened, and smiled. It was the moment that made me realize I needed to do more things like this, and not just at a conference. Students needed opportunities to be in the lead. This one experience showed that they didn't need me; they did great on their own. As much as I thought I had been teaching them, in those few hours of observing their interactions with other students, administrators, and educators from around our state, I learned about who they were beyond their identity as students in my class.

Students who rarely spoke up in class or doubted the quality of their work were proudly sharing what they had created and teaching others. That was the moment I realized that in order to provide the best learning opportunities for our students, we need to get out of their way. As uncomfortable as that may seem, and definitely unconventional compared to what has been done, the benefits can be truly great for both students and teachers.

Students have tremendous power when given an opportunity. If we limit what they are doing in our classrooms and we are their only audience, we are doing a disservice not just to them but to our school community and beyond. Preparing for the future means creating opportunities for them to connect and learn in the real world. Students need a public audience for their work, and we need to tell our stories so they can tell theirs. We must share student work and the lessons that we have learned along the way, and help students share their own stories.

QUESTIONS FOR REFLECTION

1. What experiences with failure have defined you?
2. Are there stories of your childhood or early teaching days that have led to your why?
3. Is there a student who impacted you and led you down the path to professional growth or reinforced your why?

Share it out!

How do you help others to embrace failure?

#FUTURE4EDU

Chapter 10

RISING ABOVE FAILURES

Cassy DeBacco, Student,
Riverview Junior-Senior High School

The idea that "failure is an event, not a person" is something that, as students, we lose track of all the time. We spend so much time in school. Not only are our whole academic careers there, but that's where our social life is and where we start becoming who we are. So whenever we get that bad grade on a test, or we disappoint ourselves or, even worse, we feel like we disappointed others, we are going to feel like failures. Even though it might seem silly or might not make sense to others, school really is our whole world.

Students are often defined by a letter grade, a test score, or the number of baskets scored. We are defined constantly with numbers. When a number is low and reflects failure, we will feel like a failure. That is why it is so imperative to remember that failure is an event, not a person, because students cannot be defined as a number. We are so much more than that. We have individual passions, interests, talents, strengths, and personality traits that can often never be measured with a number. If we look at failures as events, we can use those times when we fail as opportunities to grow and learn. But if we continue to see the person as the "failure" and let those failures and numbers define us, how can we ever grow?

My Struggles

I have felt like a failure so many times, on an academic level and also on a personal level. I struggle with a lot of anxiety and depression in my life. I am also a perfectionist because of the way I think. Missing even one point on a test can cause me to feel anxious and like I've disappointed others, when in reality I haven't at all. My junior year at Riverview was academically my most challenging year. I took three Advanced Placement (AP) classes, which included AP English Language, AP Chemistry, and AP History. Throughout my life I have worked hard for my grades, and my grades have always been in the high 90s. When I started getting Bs and Cs on tests, I was confused and lost. I always felt like I had learned so much in class. I studied for tests and did the hard work that many of my classmates didn't even do. However, my grades wouldn't reflect the hard work I had done or all of the knowledge I felt I had absorbed. Although I never actually failed a test, I still felt like a failure because of the high expectations I set for myself. My grades didn't reflect the effort invested or the tears I had shed over my grades. I just didn't understand. I had failed. My efforts had failed.

I had formed my whole identity from being the "smart girl" in my grade. That's how I thought others defined me, and so that's how I defined myself. Now that I was getting Bs and Cs, I wondered, "How does that reflect the 'smart girl' role I'm supposed to be playing?"

Thinking about Ziglar's quote makes me very emotional because I constantly feel like a failure in my life. For whatever reason, I put so much pressure on myself, and whenever something doesn't go perfectly, it feels like I failed. As a result, I often feel embarrassed and silly that I feel so disappointed in myself. I feel others see me as someone thriving in life, when in reality I feel like I am struggling and failing. To me, receiving a grade of a C in a class means that I have failed. It is hard for me to accept that what I feel is a failure, that my way of thinking is valid, that my feelings are valid. Although I haven't gone through the worst the world has to offer, I have definitely had my fair share of struggles.

Each mistake teaches you something new about yourself. There is no failure, remember, except in no longer trying. It is the courage to continue that counts.

—Chris Bradford

Looking Back to Move Ahead

Thinking back on all the obstacles I have tackled in my life, whenever I was in those moments, I felt despair and misery because of how much I felt like a failure. After going to therapy and experiencing more of life, I have learned that the experiences were the failure, not me. It was just a time when I struggled and that failure occurred. It wasn't me. It was just what was happening *to me*. And when I look at it that way now, I can learn from my experience. Whenever you feel like a failure, you aren't looking at a situation in a way that you can learn from; you only look back and think of the sadness or shame you might have felt. But it's almost happy looking back at an event where you failed because you've learned, you've done better, you've fixed your mistake, and you've figured out a solution. You can say, "Look where I am now."

Even in times of failure, I find strength that I didn't know I had. I can see that I pushed through difficult challenges and survived. And I can look back at those times the next time I face a challenge. After a time of failure, the slate can be wiped clean. I am a *huge* believer in second chances. And third. And fourth. And so on. If you experience an event that did not go as you would have liked, the time following that challenge is a time for new beginnings and new possibilities to fix your mistakes and try again. It's actually pretty exciting.

Failure will never overtake me if my determination to succeed is strong enough.

—Og Mandino

Failing and Growing Together

I have been able to overcome failure with help from those around me. I am blessed to have teachers who look out for my best interests, who want to see me succeed and be happy. They are there to lift me up and remind me of the reality and not the lies that I often tell myself. I wish all students were this lucky and could develop these close relationships with teachers, but I know that this is not always the case. I think it is important to be brave and reach out to someone you see as helpful and willing to give you advice. But I know some students are uncomfortable taking advice or may feel no one is there to give it to them. I am blessed to have an amazing family. Although they can frustrate me at times, I know they will always have my back and have my best interests at heart.

I realize that not every student has this kind of support either. So then what? Again, I am blessed to have friends who speak kind words into my life and remind me that I am not a failure. They help me to rise above my feelings of failure and know that I can succeed. I believe the most important thing that helped me to remember that I am not a failure, to come to these realizations and grow as a student and human being, is that I had *myself*. I had my own best interests at heart and sought help when I knew I needed it. I reached out to my guidance counselor and sought therapy. All people have themselves to lean on, and they are stronger than they think. We can seek advice and help from guidance counselors or through online chat groups, help lines, or even social media. Trust me, there are communities of people waiting to lift people's spirits up. It is so (times three) difficult to remember that failure is an event and not a person. Even though having supportive teachers, understanding parents, and uplifting friends can help us all to think positively, we help ourselves more by being kind to ourselves and seeking help when needed.

During those times when you feel alone and the failure is consuming you, when you try to remind yourself of the truth but it doesn't seem it make a difference, it is hard to push through. But if that happens—or more realistically, *when* that happens, when you feel like you tried everything and you still feel like a failure—I have learned to not shove those feelings away. Accept the fact that you feel that way and reach out for advice. Sometimes I even get upset at myself for not remembering or (more typically) not accepting the fact that failure is an event. I try to remind myself that I have gone through other struggles and challenges and have found my way through, so I can get through this obstacle too. All people are stronger than they think they are.

Where Do We Learn about Failure?

I am trying to remember where I learned the word *failure*. I am thankful my parents didn't use that word when describing my behavior as a child, because I feel like that would have been extreme and harsh. I must have learned the word *failure* from school. If you get an F, you fail a test; that is the way it works. So by that logic, the feeling of failure must have stemmed from school too. When you receive a so-called "failing grade," the feeling of shame or disappointment that results is called failure. As a student, I made the association in my brain that failure was when I received a lower grade than what I was used to. I learned to feel embarrassment and shame and fear from not performing up to the incredibly high standards I set for myself in school. As a kid, I don't remember a time when I felt like a failure as a human being, but I definitely remember feeling like a failure as a student. I believe that as I got older, and life became more complicated and messier, the separation between student and human began to fade.

As I got older and I was trying to find my identity, my identity became "the smart girl" in my grade. I think that our identity as we get older revolves around being a student because that is what our life has been based upon. Whenever I felt like I "failed" in life by not performing my best, whether that be by saying something kind of weird or by being excluded by my friends, I considered myself to be a failure. No one ever taught me the difference. No one ever taught me that I didn't have to feel awful about myself just because I got a lower grade. And no one taught me that making mistakes in life is okay and doesn't equal failure. I wish it was something that didn't have to be taught. However, the association between failure in school and failure in life is too strong, and it is inevitable that the failure taught or even learned in schools transfers to our personal lives. If we can stop using the arbitrary numbers and grades and rankings to define our intelligence, then maybe the idea of people failing will fade away. We can simply call failure an opportunity to grow and learn.

Failure is only the opportunity to begin again,
only this time more wisely.

—Henry Ford

Failures Follow You

On a bit of a sad note, failure doesn't just occur in school. I feel like I have failed my family and my friends when I have moments of depression. Whenever I feel like the world is too much and I can't go on, I feel like I've let so many people down, like I've failed my loved ones and God. I carry so much guilt because of my depression. I become ashamed of the thoughts that run through my head. Whenever I have these destructive and unhealthy thoughts, I ask myself, "Where is my evidence? What evidence do I have for feeling like a failure?" No one is telling me that I have been a disappointment. Even the Bible gives me evidence that I am loved! This helps me to remember that I am not a failure, and remembering that failure is an event saves me from having more depressing thoughts. I can look back on those times of despair and see them as an opportunity to learn from sometimes irrational and unhealthy ways of thinking.

Often when we as humans are rude or unkind to one another, we feel—or we are told—that we failed. I wish that whenever we have our moments of unkindness towards others that we weren't labeled a certain way. If those moments of unkindness or failure are events, then we can learn from them and move on. But if we are defined by those moments of failure, if we are called "failures" because we said something mean to someone when we were having a bad day, how can we ever let go of grudges and be kind to each other in the future? How can we learn from those moments of weakness and become better people? How can we change if we are labeled as failures?

Having moments of unkindness to others does not mean we fail at being good people or fail at being human, because all humans make mistakes. People are perfectly imperfect. We are supposed to make mistakes so we can learn and grow from them.

> If the purpose for learning is to score well on a test, we've lost sight of the real reason for learning.
> —Jeannie Fulbright

More Than a Number

As a student, I absolutely hate getting a grade on a test. I am not a number. I am not defined by one arbitrary test or assignment. I've learned as I get older that As and Bs don't define me. I am so much more than what's on paper. If you look at "me" on paper, you can say that I failed or that I wasn't good enough, but I wouldn't change a thing because those events have made me who I am today.

I understand that there has to be a way to numerically determine if we are learning in school. But I wish there was another way to do it besides giving us points and grades and marking up papers with red pens, because those times of failing in school can be so traumatic and detrimental because *we* feel like failures. Whenever I get a bad grade, it often deflates my confidence. I am continually feeling let down with myself. When I go into the test, I often feel more anxious and fearful and that reflects in my test grade, and the cycle continues.

I am someone who wants to *earn* my grade. I don't cheat or pretend that I learned something when I really haven't. I wish all grades were determined with objectives. We use this method in my physics classes. We are given either a "developing mastery" or "mastery," on each objective covered in class, and then the opportunity to reassess on any objective to earn mastery where it has not already been attained. Mastery-based grading is different, but I believe it to be a very effective way of grading. Students take quizzes but do not receive a letter grade. Instead, the questions on the quiz are associated with a learning objective, a topic or a concept learned in class. The students can either receive a "no-evidence" (if the student had not answered the question), a "developing mastery" (if the student had not answered the questions relating to that objective correctly) or a "mastery" (if the student had answered questions relating to that objective correctly and demonstrated understanding of that objective). Then, the students are able to reassess on any objective they received an NE (no-evidence) or a DM (developing mastery) on. The benefit is that it gives the students the chance to complete extra practice and then earn a mastery in any objective by retaking a test. A letter grade is determined based on the number of mastery indicators a student has and how they score on an end of the semester test. This way of grading really shows what the student knows. Any student can start the year with all NEs but do the hard work and end with mastery and an A in the class. It is a great representation of true learning for students because we are not *given* points, we *earn* our grades. This method of learning seems fair and much more reflective of my skills and knowledge as a learner.

However, to be honest, I know from experience that many students would not like this method of grading, because we use it in my school district. Students would rather have an A (by the way, what does that even mean?) than to feel they have learned something. If given the choice, most students would rather be *given* a 100 percent than *earning* an 80 percent. I am the opposite. It's hard for me to have a solution for a different way of determining learning, when I know that many of my peers wouldn't feel the same.

But maybe if we stop with the points, we can stop associating learning with numbers. Instead, we can start associating learning with students.

> There is no failure except in no longer trying.
> —Elbert Hubbard

Failure Is an Event...

The Ziglar quote says "remember." I want to encourage everyone to think carefully about this quote. Remember that *you* are not a failure, that failures are things that happen to us. Always remind yourself,

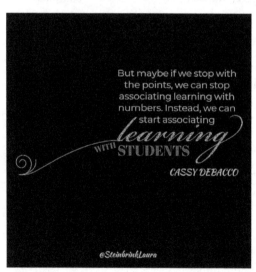

But maybe if we stop with the points, we can stop associating learning with numbers. Instead, we can start associating *learning* WITH **STUDENTS**

CASSY DEBACCO

@SteinbrinkLaura

as you reflect on your past or hope for the future, that failures do not define you. *You* are not a failure. You may be "failing" by others' definition, but you are not defined by what happens to you, but rather by how you handle what happens to you. And failures are just what happens to you.

If and when failure happens, try not to give up and get discouraged. Try not to feel the shame and embarrassment that can often come along with failure. Keep on going and keep on trying.

> Our greatest success is not in never failing,
> but in rising every time we fail.
> —Confucius

Cassy DeBacco is a senior at Riverview High School in Oakmont, PA. She is involved in many clubs, such as National Honor Society, Students Against Destructive Decisions, Key Club, Spanish Club and student council, and she holds multiple leadership roles. Cassy is also involved in varsity tennis, plays the viola in many groups, and volunteers her time as a youth ministry leader. She has presented at edtech conferences such as TRETC and PETE&C. After high school, she plans to continue her education with a major in mathematics.

QUESTIONS FOR REFLECTION

1. How can we encourage students to ask for help when they need it? What are some strategies to create those connections?
2. Can you identify some students who might be experiencing the same thing as Cassy? How can her story help them?
3. What are steps that you can take tomorrow to spread the message that failure is an event, not a person?

SHARE IT OUT!

Make an affirmation about failure and tweet to **#FUTURE4EDU.**

Part III

GATHERING STRENGTH AND GLADIATING TOGETHER

Chapter 11

BREAKING TRADITIONS: LEARNING ADVENTURES AND TEACHERPRENEURS

Too often we give children answers to remember rather than
problems to solve.

—Roger Lewin

Things have changed so much in education. I experience
some of the transformations as they are happening, but even still, sometimes
change is still shocking to me. For those who have not been in a classroom
or don't keep up with the new trends in education, the current landscape
of education likely looks completely different than what they experienced
as students. Unlike years ago, we have access to more tools and resources
than we ever have. It's understandable why some educators might prefer
to keep with the tried-and-true traditional methods they've always used.
Having folders full of worksheets, stacks of books, and other supplementary
materials, many of which do not involve technology, might be a lot more
comfortable and easier to keep up with than worrying about finding time to
learn the latest tool or trying a new method.

Lack of direction, not lack of time, is the problem. We all
have twenty-four-hour days.

—Zig Ziglar

We Make Time for What's Important

How can we find enough time to know what new ideas are out there
and which we should explore? It takes having a plan, setting your mind to do
something; if it is important, then we make time for it. Finding time to ask
questions or having time to sit and carry on a conversation with colleagues
would be difficult on most days. However, knowing the potential that could be
gained by gathering data, it made sense to me to create an educator survey and
post it on Twitter to gather feedback and learn from a variety of people with
different experiences and perspectives. The results? A common concern was
finding enough time to complete all of the responsibilities, besides actually
teaching, that take extra planning and organization. I feel like it increases
every year, with new initiatives introduced or changes made to the different
technologies we use in our schools. It's understandable why teachers might
prefer to save time by using what they already have, rather than creating
something entirely new. But it's important that we stay relevant and current.
We need to find ways to stay motivated so that we don't stay with the status
quo, placing limits on ourselves—but more importantly and most critically,
we must remember that by limiting ourselves, we limit our students. We need
to break away from what is most comfortable and easiest for us, and instead
explore innovative ways to teach our classes that will engage students and
offer more authentic ways for students to connect with the content.

Changes will be constant, and to keep up with them we need to be innovative and willing to expand our own skills. Our responsibility is to model lifelong
learning and constantly work on improving our own practice. If we are not

willing to do this, then how can we expect our students to take risks in learning or to develop the initiative to advocate for their own needs? Being stagnant in our own growth will negatively affect our students. We are leaders in the classroom, and it starts with us. We must be willing to bring about changes and to model risk-taking. When we do this, we show students how we deal with setbacks when they happen, how to engage in reflective practice, and how to work toward a goal. We must emphasize the process of learning involved and not the product. By focusing less on earning points or simply completing something to "get it done," and more on learning throughout the whole process, failures and successes included, we will help students to develop a growth mindset.

Would You Want to Be Your Own Student?

Stop and think about the classroom experience you are providing for students. Do you take time to engage in conversations with students and ask for their feedback? How often do you reflect on the methods you use? It is important to get feedback from others, but we also need evaluate ourselves. Think carefully about your classroom environment and then ask yourself two very important questions. First, from Dave Burgess, author of *Teach Like a Pirate*, "If your students didn't have to be there, would you be teaching to an empty room?"[1] Second, from George Couros, author of *The Innovator's Mindset*, "Would you want to be a learner in your own classroom?"[2] Using these questions as a guide, consider the types of experiences you are creating for your students. Are they engaged, involved in class discussions and decisions, and do they have choices? Do students have opportunities to co-design the learning activities or is your classroom still teacher-centered and teacher-driven?

1   Burgess, Dave. (2012). *Teach Like A Pirate*. pg. 58. San Diego, CA: DAVE BURGESS CONSULTING.

2   Couros, G. (2015). *The Innovator's Mindset: Empower Learning, Unleash Talent, and Lead a Culture of Creativity*. pg. 49. San Diego, CA: Dave Burgess Consulting

I never thought about what it might feel like being a student in my class, and I did not ask students. I pretty much just started each class the way that I wanted to start. I planned the activities, assigned the homework, and proceeded through every lesson using as many of the minutes in the period as I could, without asking for any student input. And honestly it never occurred to me that I could or should. But over the past five or six years, I started to ask because I really wanted to know what they thought. At times I created surveys to gather their thoughts. I wanted the feedback and hoped that students would feel comfortable telling me the good and the bad.

One thing I've noticed about students, especially some of the younger students I have taught, is that they can be brutally honest at times. You might want to be careful what you ask them if you're not prepared for the answers they might give. I've had some surprising answers, but if you are looking for honest feedback, which may be good or bad or somewhere in between, then you need to ask and prepare to listen closely to what they say.

School Is Boring?

One of the most common responses I hear from students is that everything is "boring." Every class and every period. Every day is pretty much the same for them: sit, listen, take notes, take a test, look at PowerPoint presentations for most of the period. There are not many opportunities to move around, to collaborate with peers, to do something *different*. Students often say classes are boring but then quickly add, "Oh, but not your class," in an effort to not hurt my feelings. It makes me laugh because I can see their reactions to having said "every class," and when their eyes make contact with me, I can always tell they feel a little uncomfortable, thinking they might have offended me. They don't. Honestly, I hear that things are boring a lot, from students in my class and from students talking about their other classes. I use this as a teachable moment.

I always start by letting them know that it's okay to tell me because I can't make changes unless I know. We talk about there being a right way and a wrong way to provide feedback and how to express our feelings in a kind, respectful way, especially if they might be a little critical of someone or something. The more I have asked students for feedback, and stay open to their ideas, the better I feel about providing a student-centered classroom and taking some risks with change.

Breaking the Plan, Breaking Tradition

We need to change from what we have always done. Each class should offer unique learning experiences for students, rather than having them be part of a repetitive routine for learning. If we set a goal to think differently and involve students in creating a learning adventure rather than the traditional lesson, a whole world of possibilities opens up. It might be scary to try, but what is the worst that could happen if you say to students, "Today we need to practice [name the content]," and give them a period of time, say ten or fifteen minutes, to come up with their own ways to practice, whether in small groups or with a partner. Use that time to observe how they are interacting and working together on an idea, and listen to how they are communicating and brainstorming. We can always learn from our students. Keep in mind that the first time may be a little rough, especially if students use the opportunity to socialize rather than stay on task. Set up some guidelines to remind them that it's not simply a time to socialize, although learning is social and students should have opportunities to interact with their classmates. The first time trying this will give you a chance to listen to what students are coming up with and consider their ideas as having applicability to the whole class and what the benefits might be. I have done this, and I guarantee that you will have a lot of insight into the students and their interests, and learn unique and authentic ideas for practicing the content.

Be a Teacherpreneur

A teacherpreneur is not afraid to diverge from the traditional methods, to abandon a lesson plan in favor of a student's creative way to engage with the content, or to expand on something a student said that became a teachable moment. There is not a classroom out there that has not had a student, or several students, lead the discussion off-topic, sometimes almost daily. It's what happens next that makes the difference. Teachers can decide to stop the conversation, react adversely, and possibly further interrupt the learning, or instead think about how to use it to push learning further. A teacherpreneur will find ways to incorporate these diversions into the lesson somehow and use them as preparation for future lessons.

Be Willing to Break Traditions

A teacherpreneur is not afraid to take chances in the classroom and works to bring unique, engaging learning experiences to students. Traditionally, students spend a lot of time passively learning in classrooms, sitting in the same assigned seats, working independently, repeating similar learning activities throughout their school day. It's time to make some changes to empower students with more opportunities to collaborate, to build relationships and foster peer connections in the classroom. Lee Vygotsky, a Russian teacher and psychologist, is credited with first stating that we learn through interactions with our peers and teachers. Social learning theory explains how people learn in different social contexts and how creating a more active learning community can positively impact a learner's ability and better meet individual learner goals.[3]

---

3   The Hechinger Report. (2019). Working in a group might be the best way to help kids meet individual goals, study says - The Hechinger Report. [online] Available at: https://hechingerreport.org/working-in-a-group-might-be-the-best-way-to-help-kids-meet-individual-goals-study-says/.

About two years ago, I had been struggling with the level of student engagement and reached out to my PLN for ideas. After trying a few suggestions like using different technology tools, moving away from daily homework, and designing better projects that gave students more choices in learning, the improvements that I had hoped for did not happen. My next step was taking time to talk with my students, ask for some ideas, and step away from being the only one teaching in the classroom. There were slight improvements, but I realized that I needed to make bigger changes. I looked at my classroom one morning and did not like how it looked. Rigid, structured, fixed. I made the decision to break apart the rows of desks, and instead created "stations" of three or four desks so that I could promote more interactive learning experiences. I wanted to be more available to my students and to create a more collaborative and innovative learning space for them. Moving away from the front of the classroom and having students decide where to sit at times was a little uncomfortable in the beginning. In my mind I had imagined my classroom becoming a chaotic space.

At first, it can be a challenge to transition from the traditional classroom instruction you may be using, but it only takes that first step to see the benefits that the changes will bring. Give students more opportunities to design learning activities like games, or to create lessons with technology tools, or even come up with their own ideas for how to practice new content. More social learning full of student choice equates to a more meaningful experience for students, as well as better content retention and increased motivation. Being open to student ideas, making time to explore new options, and taking their suggestions can lead to a more authentic learning experience. Once I let go a little and took some risks in our classroom, I noticed my students started to ask more questions like, "Can we...?" "What if...?" "Is it okay to...?" They even suggested improvements: "Maybe we could..." "It might be better if we..." and, "This has helped me to remember...can we keep doing these activities?" They surprised me and I surprised myself.

My answer to their questions was, "Yes, I think we should try it." In twenty years of teaching, I had never taken steps like this. I was curious if their ideas would work and how we could all benefit from doing things differently. Was I worried? A bit, but that's always a part of the risk. My curiosity outweighed my fear of taking a risk because I had tried different strategies and they had not worked. Since then, my motto has been: "If it works, then great. And if not, *we* will try again!"

> Part of education is learning. And what drives learning is curiosity and collaboration.
>
> —Sir Ken Robinson

Curiosity and Wonder

When I was about ten years old, I had a cousin who was probably around two, and her favorite word was *why*. No matter what people would say or what she would see people doing, she questioned *everything*. Even if you gave her an answer, she would still continue to ask why after each response given. And simply saying "because" was not enough. I did not understand why she did this, so I typically lost patience with her after probably the seventh or eighth time that she questioned me (remember, I was only ten) and tried my best to get her to stop. I often made up answers because I didn't know why the sky was blue or where the moon hid all day, and hoped that I would give her an answer that just might be the one, but it never really worked. The only thing that helped was finding something else to distract her, but it was only a temporary solution because she would see something and then start all over again by asking, "Why?"

When I think about children of that age or close to it, I've heard that many tend to ask that same question. I don't have children of my own, and so I don't know if it's just the age or if it's the natural progression in the cognitive development of a child. I have read that questioning peaks at the age of four, and on average, a four-year-old child asks around 400 questions per week.[4] Wow! Of course, I didn't realize this when I was younger and never gave it much thought after that, but thinking back to that time, and also considering other children I have been around, I can see that the sense of wonder in children is amazing. They have such curiosity for the world around them and continue to question everything and want to know why. It's not enough to know the answer; they search for a deeper meaning, getting behind the why.

CURIOSITY IN CHILDREN
IS BUT AN APPETITE
FOR KNOWLEDGE.
JOHN LOCKE

@MANUELHERRERA33

Kate Lindquist, Elementary Art Teacher (K–5), West Palm Beach, Florida, @heARTISTatWORK

What happens when we impose too many rules? And taking that one step further, how does that affect education?

Being an elementary school art teacher affords me the opportunity to look at these two questions in a few unique ways. In one way, I

---

4   Emma Elsworthy, "Curious Children Ask 73 Questions Each Day—Many of Which Parents Can't Answer, Says Study," Independent, December 3, 2017, https://www.independent.co.uk/news/uk/home-news/curious-children-questions-parenting-mum-dad-google-answers-inquisitive-argos-toddlers-chad-valley-a8089821.html.

am privileged (and honestly blessed) to see eight hundred students from different backgrounds, with various stories, learning styles, academic abilities, and wildly unique personalities. But recently, as I have been observing them in the art room for a mere thirty minutes every eight days, I am noticing something disheartening: they lack creativity and curiosity. They have been with their classroom teacher all day following a multitude of rules. When students first enter the art room, they are unable to access the part of the brain that is flowing with creativity and curiosity.

"What do you mean I can have choices in how I add color to my project?" As the period passes by and I continue to throw what-ifs, "how comes," and out-of-the-box ideas at them, all of a sudden magic happens! They become alive! They become curious! They become creative little geniuses that astound me. Yes, rules are necessary. But when too many are imposed upon us, our creative and curious brains shut down.

I'm not sure if some of us are born with an extra dose of creativity and curiosity (I have plenty to share if you need some) or if some of us just never outgrow the "why" stage of a two-year-old. I love the quote by Twyla Tharp: "Creativity is an act of defiance. You're challenging the status quo. You're questioning accepted truths and principles."

If we want to create lifelong learners as well as lifelong educators, we might want to think about loosening the "rule reins" just a bit.

●●●

Staying Constantly Curious

We can learn a lot from the curiosity of young minds, but somewhere along the way, that sense of wonder and curiosity fades and sometimes even disappears as we get older. I see less and less curiosity shown by students each year. I'm not sure why it happens, but for some reason, people stop feeling comfortable asking why and questioning things, like it is wrong to question. There are times when I still feel myself tense up when asked even a simple question, and it has always been this way. When I am questioned, I sometimes interpret the question to mean that I must be wrong, or that my skills are being evaluated. As an educator, I have not always been comfortable with being questioned about what I am teaching and why, and more recently I've had students ask me why they have to learn something in class. Initially it felt like they were challenging *me*. I interpreted their questions to be asking why I was choosing to teach in a certain way or use a particular teaching method, as if suggesting that I was teaching the wrong way. But then I realized they were mostly just curious. They wondered when they would use the information and what the benefit was to them of learning different things in our class. Why learn something just for the sake of learning it? I can relate this back to when I was a student. There were things I learned that I could not imagine ever using (and hoped that I wouldn't need to) but still did what I was "supposed" to do, what I had been told to do, without ever thinking to ask my teachers for any reason behind it. And definitely not pushing back as much as what I have experienced over the past few years in my own classes.

Now I've become more mindful of sharing the why behind what students are learning. I give the purpose from the start, almost in anticipation of the occasional grunts and groans about doing work. The alternative, ignoring their questions, would mean that I would be contributing to the loss of wonder and curiosity. Sometimes I need to have a discussion with students about the right way to question things, because without a little guidance, some of their curiosity might come across as confrontational and would not be very well received. I remember how I interpreted it when I didn't know better.

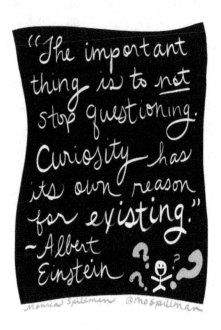

"The important thing is to not stop questioning. Curiosity has its own reason for existing." ~Albert Einstein

Monica Spillman @mospillman

We need to help students stay curious and further develop their sense of wonder, not be afraid to ask others why and, even more importantly, to ask themselves why. Think about answers to the questions: Why are we doing something, why do we hope to make some change, and why should our students be invested? We can't and shouldn't simply accept something because that means compliance. We have to keep exploring to find new ways to learn and to stretch ourselves.

- Be curious, because that is when learning happens.
- Be okay with failing, because that is when progress is made.
- Be vulnerable, because that is when others see who you are.
- Be willing to take a chance and make a change for good.

BE CURIOUS.
BE OKAY WITH FAILING.
BE VULNERABLE.
BE WILLING
TO TAKE A CHANCE.

Questions for Reflection

1. How can you break from being the only leader in the classroom?
2. What is one thing about teaching that you would change?
3. When you try new ideas and they don't go well, how do you recover and start again?

SHARE IT OUT!

Add your one thing to the hashtag **#FUTURE4EDU.**

Chapter 12

LEARNING FROM LIFE
FOR THE FUTURE

Don't limit a child to your own learning,
for he was born in another time.

—Rabindranath Tagore

One of the most important responsibilities of educators is to pursue lifelong learning. By the nature of our work and the ever-changing world, we must actively seek new knowledge and pursue personal and professional growth. We must be invested in ourselves so that we are prepared to provide the most relevant, authentic, and purposeful learning experiences for our students. We can do this by opening doors for them to pursue their own interests, guiding them only at the start, and letting them explore and even struggle on their own. Sometimes we might need to build a door to help them get started. We are all learners in the classroom. If we simply keep teaching the same content, limited to our knowledge alone, we limit students' potential for continued growth and can even take away their opportunity to become curious for learning. We need students to become curious, to innovate, and to dream for the future.

The teaching profession and the skills required have evolved tremendously over the past five years, and sometimes it feels like I can't keep up with the trends. To help myself learn more, I used the survey I created and shared on Twitter. I included questions asking educators what they considered to be the most important topics in education, buzzwords, skills and traits of teachers today. I also asked for ideas about how to start each school year. The most common trends in education listed were blended and flipped learning, differentiation, growth mindset, social-emotional learning, project-based learning, restorative practices, and trauma-informed teaching. As for characteristics that educators should have, the most frequent responses were grit, perseverance, resilience, tenacity, and mindfulness. These are qualities and traits that we need to embody today in our role as educators and model for those we lead.

Has It Always Been This Way?

Think back to when you were a student. Can you identify any learning experiences related to these concepts? Did teachers talk about having grit or developing a growth mindset? Did you have teachers who encouraged you to keep trying, learn from mistakes made, and keep pushing yourself to grow? Did they challenge you to push through the struggle of learning? Or was learning viewed and experienced as a single, final event? A test was taken, graded, returned, and then you moved on to the next topic or chapter.

The majority of my learning activities and assessments in both elementary and high school were more of an "over and done" experience. I recall getting tests back from my teachers, often covered in red marks, sometimes with correct answers written in or a few comments made. Other times we might go over the questions in class or receive an answer key, but there were very few opportunities to have individual discussions with a teacher. As for communication to parents, there was not much shared between school and home other than during grading periods, and I don't recall having opportunities to retake a quiz. An F was still an F, and even if I did all of the homework (which I did) and participated, the tests were my weakest area. I got some Ds and Fs, and they really impacted my confidence, but I don't believe that my grades truly reflected my understanding of the content. We need to think about how we assess and what those grades mean for learning and student development.

Opportunities to Learn from Mistakes

In order to thrive, students need to be supported in school and at home. By communicating often with families, we create the supportive relationships that students need and engage families more in the learning experience of the students. Keeping families informed about student progress is critical, and the communication exchanged should include positives and negatives. We should inform families of strengths and make them aware of areas that are in progress. There are diverse methods for doing this today through technology for sharing student work, sending a quick message, and interacting in a virtual space. When I was a student in elementary school, there were many times when I had to take papers home for my parents to sign because I received a low grade, typically a low C or below. My parents would try to explain what I had done wrong, and often they would help me to understand why I had missed something. There are still old homework assignments, tests, and projects stored in boxes at my parents' house that I have occasionally looked at to remember my student experience. Why? Because I want to compare methods, see if I am using similar practices in my classroom today, and see how much I remember about the content, especially when I received a bad grade in a class.

Give More Than a Grade

What I have noticed is that sometimes the comments were less focused on positives or giving encouraging feedback. There were not suggestions on how to get the right answer but rather things like "Wrong," "What???" or "Try harder," and there were times when my teacher had written "Didn't you study???" on my test, or there was the large letter grade of a C, D, or even a large cursive F, circled in red ink. I grew to really dislike the red pen, always anticipating the worst as papers were returned if I could see any sign of red ink. It didn't make me feel good about my work or myself, and to me, it immediately represented failure. It was easy to see who had done well and who had not, which made it even more uncomfortable.

High school was mostly the same; many teachers graded the same—red ink, big circled letter grades—but there were more conversations between teachers and students. I recall a few teachers who took time to have a quick conversation with students and explain the errors. It made a difference to us as students when we knew teachers valued the importance of relationships and were invested in our progress.

The first few years I taught, I used my own assessment experiences and crafted my own way to grade and give feedback. For many years, my practice was similar to what I had experienced as a student. Looking back now, I realize that I was not doing what I should have been. My experience should have led me to do something different.

> Forgive yourself for not having the foresight to know what
> now seems so obvious in hindsight.
>
> —Judy Belmont

Jon Craig, Instructional Coach, Harry S. Truman High School, Bristol Township School District, @coachjoncraig

In 2016, I entered my sixth year of teaching AP American History and was finally beginning to feel comfortable with the content, pace, and challenges of the rigorous course. My students' success had grown steadily over those first five years, so I felt that only minor tweaks were needed to improve instruction and learning in my class. Those days were filled with teacher-driven lessons of lecture and limited student discussion, while students were mostly passive in the classroom. However, that year felt different.

Students were struggling more than usual with the content and course demands, and worse, they seemed less engaged than ever. Additionally, I was feeling stale, even bored, with the day-to-day routine, and it felt like I was failing my students. I had to find another way.

I had just started a Twitter account, and as I began connecting with educators, I stumbled across flipped instruction. I loved the concept and how it placed students in control of their learning, so I dove in head first. Although there were bumps on the road, I felt the culture begin to change in my classroom. I wanted to innovate. Someone told me to go see George Couros at a local conference, so I did. His message and keynote changed my views further. I wanted to change more about my instruction. I came across "genius hour" through Couros's work and other educators, and I wanted to provide that learning opportunity for my students. The experience was academically compelling. Things would never be the same in my classroom again.

The relationships and culture we built for personalized learning in that classroom were all the evidence I needed to never go back to my prior approaches. My failure was a gift. It pushed me to innovate, connect, and always reflect on my practice. Whether it's a new instructional method, mindset, or something else, we should not fear change. We can learn from our struggles and failures. It is all part of the learning process. Response to failure is how we grow.

•••

Why We Need to Change

During my first roughly twenty years of teaching, when it came to assessments, class activities, or homework, I am not proud to say that I used some of the same practices and grading policies that my own teachers had. I used to teach the way that I was taught. I didn't know anything different, and it mostly worked for me as a student. We had homework every night that was collected or checked for completion. Some teachers had us correct the work of our peers. If you did not do the homework, you received a zero, and there were very few opportunities to hand it in late for partial credit.

I've shared my struggle with grades with my own students. There were a lot of tests, many that I received very low grades on. I struggled so much in my ninth-grade geometry class. I studied every night and reviewed with my dad, but I was lost during class and failed most every test I took. For the first three grading periods, I received an F, a D, and another F. It was not that I didn't understand the content; I did. I could explain theorems, give examples, and solve problems, except during tests or pop quizzes. The yellow half-sheets of paper came back covered in red ink and writing I could not even read, but the message was very clear: I failed. I did not know what I was doing. Geometry was going to be very difficult. I was going to get an F. And I did, more than once. Failure.

"Our greatest weakness lies in giving up. The most certain way to succeed is always try just one more time." -Thomas Edison

Debbie Holman, Science Teacher, Science Department Head, Wellington, Colorado, @debbiejholman

The moment I learned about gamification, I knew it was an experience I wanted to create for students in my eighth-grade science classes. I'd included games in the learning experience before, but never as a year-long adventure. Imagining students engaging in game elements as a way to deliver content was exciting, fun, and novel!

The first year, I gave badges for showing proficiency on standards. I thought this game element would be an excellent motivator. At first it was, but students soon became bored with it. Like my sticker-book collection in the eighties, it was super fun, but after a while there wasn't anything new, so I got bored and lost interest. This is what happened that first year. I hadn't created a consistent way to track the paper badges, nor was there a good way for students who missed badges to catch up. Besides being a colorful display on their notebooks, the badges were meaningless. I continued to give the colorful badges for most of the year, but I did not finish the year with them. It was not what I had hoped for.

During the second year, I added additional elements to the game and continued to hand out badges. Students collected these items and exchanged them for other items such as getting dibs on a special chair or exploring with the thermal imaging camera if they finished early. I soon realized that this was not gamifying. Students were sharing, bartering, and selling their items but not connecting with the content or the game. I had created only a token economy, which felt like another forced thing for students to participate in and not the type of gamification I read about in the book *Explore Like a Pirate* by Michael Matera. I got my book out and joined a book study on Voxer during the summer. Being able to discuss the ideas from the book with others who were also struggling enabled me to work through the things I was not understanding about gamifying my own classroom.

It's the third year of this journey, and my students are now engaged in a game called Chaos. They gain experience points by engaging in the narrative using a website that has training missions, quests, and a badging system all connected to the narrative and the science content that I teach. Students have become interested in helping to design the game, which promotes student ownership in learning the content and game play. I am transparent with students by letting them know that it is a work in progress. They know when I make a mistake, and they help me to problem solve and work through the issue. Being transparent when failure occurs in the classroom becomes a learning opportunity not only for me as a teacher, guide, and mentor, but for the learners in my care. It is an opportunity to see how failure can lead to success.

In my classroom we embrace, celebrate, and look for ways to fail even if it means that we don't finish the learning target or get through all of the material. Although it is disappointing to not get it right the first time, I am not afraid. It allows us to learn more by experiencing and growing from our failures as a result of the risks we take. I am a failure, and I own that proudly. I fail each day and still get up, reflect, and game on!

• • •

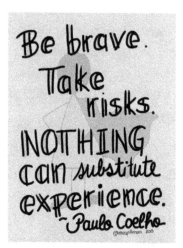

What Failures Can Teach Us

As educators, I think we are often viewed as experts of our content, people who must have all been good students, with good grades, who loved school. My reason for thinking this is that over the years, there have been so many times that students will comment that I probably never got a bad grade and didn't understand what it meant to get a D or an F. Even in the content area that I teach, there are assumptions that I know everything. I don't. I wasn't always a great student, and did not always get good grades, and although I played school a lot, I did not always love school. But what this helps me to do is to put myself in the place of my students, and it reminds me to make sure that I encourage them, that I share my own failures and how I pushed through them, and why it made a difference. I always think back to ninth-grade geometry, the first class that I got lower than a C, which for me was like failing. I wanted to quit and felt helpless for a long time. But I didn't give up. With nowhere to go but up, I figured out how to study better and started to understand geometry more. Although I did get one D and two Fs, I got an A for each of the remaining three grading periods and ended with a C average, which was good enough for me. I didn't fail. I'm not too sure what I did differently, or if the fear of failing again was so strong that it somehow gave me clarity when it came to geometry. It may be hard to believe, but geometry ended up being one of my favorite classes. I enjoyed the teacher and her quirky methods, and every day was a fun learning adventure—except when it came to grades.

I have not used geometry much, except to help my students, but somehow, over thirty years later, I still remember a lot of what I learned (in spite of failing for half of the year). So what is the lesson we learn from failures, and what does that say about the meaning of grades? I learned that giving up is the easy thing to do. I can use my experience to empathize with students who are experiencing what I did, make a connection with them that will show that I do understand because I survived the failing grades, and that I won't give up on them in my classroom, and I won't let them give up either.

How did it impact me moving forward in the decisions I make as a teacher? It gives me a different lens to view students through in my classroom. A reminder that what worked for me may not work for my students. It reminds me of a quote by Ignacio Estrada that one of my students actually referred to a few years ago without even knowing about the quote. Estrada said, "If a child can't learn the way we teach, maybe we should teach the way they learn." How can we better understand our students' needs?

Experience Informs Practice

Think of an experience in a class that you struggled with. Did you try everything you could, but your efforts still resulted in a less-than-stellar grade? Did you reach out to your teacher for help? If so, what was the impact on your learning? And if not, why didn't you? Now shift your thinking to the students in your own classroom. Are there students who might be having an experience similar to yours or mine? What are you doing to reach those students and help them to be successful? What did your experience teach you about how to provide for your students? Be the teacher you had or become the one that you needed.

We need to be keenly aware of the needs of our students and monitor their performance in class. I strongly believe it should be a priority to know exactly where our students are in terms of learning, their comfort level, and the background knowledge they bring. Our understanding develops through relationships starting on day one, and by working on them every day throughout the year. Make time for the moments; even the slightest interactions will make a difference. Students need to connect with you in order to connect with the content you are teaching. If you don't feel like you have a good understanding of where students are in the learning process, that's okay because you can start tomorrow. We always have room to grow.

"You only fail when you stop trying."

As a high school student getting Fs in geometry, on English reading comprehension quizzes, or in my physics class, I felt like a failure. I tried, struggled, and failed. Maybe I could have studied more, but the lesson I was learning was that sometimes it didn't matter what I did. When I was a young child, not doing well was something that I didn't understand. I thought that failing a test meant that I myself was a failure. I put a lot of effort into my work and tried, but the end result was that I still failed. Failing led me to believe that I was the failure because I could not complete the task no matter what I had done. But I never gave up. I have used my experiences to encourage students to keep trying. Sometimes I tell the story about the late Rita Pierson, who said, "Every kid needs a champion," and share how she encouraged a student in her math class. When a student taking a test had missed eighteen out of twenty questions, she wrote a +2 for the grade. Why? She said because that looks better than a -18 and it tells the student "you got two right and are on your way." Always lift students up, show the positive and show the possibilities.

Don't Let Failures Slow You Down

We have to create a culture of learning and growing together. We need to foster a culture for students and ourselves where we not only celebrate our successes and strengths, but also embrace the failures, and we do this together. Sharing this is so important because we know that when we fail, it's not just an opportunity to improve ourselves and do better, but it is a way to show others that it's okay to make a mistake, to fall down, and to struggle. It is what we decide to do afterward that defines us. Where do we go from that failure? We should not be embarrassed or withdraw at all. Failures are expected, encouraged even, because that is when true learning happens. In life there will be challenges, and we have to prepare our students to be able to handle the bumps on their learning journey and to push past and even celebrate failures as part of the learning process and preparation for life. In the book *Pure Genius* by Don Wettrick, he stated that students have to learn how to fail, struggle, and try again. We are tasked with preparing students for the real world, and it "is not a place where all problems have correct answers and are found in a textbook."[1]

Dennis Griffin, Principal, Brown Deer, Wisconsin, @D4Griffin[3]

Sleepless nights. Setbacks. Reflection. Training. Doubt. Learning. Failure. Perseverance. Determination. Time and time again, I find myself in admiration of the skill sets and talents of masters when their craft is on full display. Masters of a craft display an artistry in motion that captivates, inspires, and establishes a bar of excellence for others to ascend to. Ericsson, Krampe, and Tesch-Römer stated that it takes ten thousand deliberate hours on one task in order to achieve the status of mastery.[2] Ten thousand hours! The title of mastery is often not obtained because it is the unique mix of gifts, hard work, failure, learning, and perseverance. What happens during those ten thousand hours of deliberate practice?

In my journey, I have discovered that many people confuse the artistry in motion with the absence of failure and desire to achieve instant gratification from their journeys. I often wonder what events shaped the mastery that we have garnered. How much time did Michael Jordan, Lebron James, and Aaron Rodgers spend on the mastery of their craft? I wonder if they even consider themselves to be masters or dedicated workers? Mastery comes with failures, setbacks, doubts, trials, and tribulations. The real artistry in mastery is in the journey of overcoming failure and growing into your version of the master. When educators become masters,

---

1   Wettrick, Don. *Pure Genius: Building a Culture of Innovation and Taking 20% Time to the next Level.* San Diego, CA: Dave Burgess Consulting, 2014. pg. 128.

2   K. Anders Ericsson, Ralf T. Krampe, and Clemens Tesch-Römer, "The Role of Deliberate Practice in the Acquisition of Expert Performance," Psychological Review 100, no. 3 (July 1993): 363–406, https://psycnet.apa.org/doi/10.1037/0033-295X.100.3.363.

they have the unique opportunity to take what they have learned and light the paths of mastery of their students' futures.

●●●

Success is the ability to go from one failure to another with no loss of enthusiasm.

—Winston Churchill

Matthew Larson, Vice Principal, Millville Public Charter School, Millville NJ, @mlarson_nj

I had an established program. I had professional respect. I had tenure. I had two jobs and a rental house, family support within driving distance, and decade-old friends in town. Then I didn't.

In 2014, I left a tenured position after paying off my North Carolina Teaching Fellows service debt to pursue a new chapter in New Jersey with my young family. Before I left North Carolina, I looked up every school district in New Jersey and their vacancies and applied to every single position available. Every. Single. One.

Zero calls.

There I was driving into New Jersey the day after my school let out with no job prospects or leads and no living space of my own.

The phone rang. It was an interview opportunity in North Jersey at a charter school! The day came and went . . . no call back. Failed. Another phone call for a charter school in Philadelphia! I drove ninety minutes to the school and delivered a great lesson with minimal equipment in a half-clean cafeteria . . . no call back. Failed.

During all of this, I was able to find a position at a local gym franchise selling memberships to provide for a young family and save something, anything, to get us into our own place. Apparently I wasn't a great salesman. I got moved to personal training making less money. Failed.

Each failure is an iteration closer to success. Finally there came a break, albeit a small one, as I got a call for an interview at a Catholic school for a part-time position. I felt like I nailed it and I finally was right! That elusive teaching contract was finally found and signed. I still needed to work my personal training job to supplement my income, and I ended up finding another part-time job online, which provided flexibility in schedule and a few extra bucks each month. Oh, by the way, October came, and we found out the Catholic school was closing indefinitely at the end of the year after sixty-plus years in existence. Back to the grind I went.

Today I have been in my teaching position for four years and am on the hunt for the right school fit for an administrative role. Seven district interviews. Seven rejections. Each failure is an iteration closer to success. So I keep iterating to succeed.

●●●

Neither failure, nor feeling like a failure, are things we outgrow after high school. There have been times in my adult life when I have really struggled, like in law school, trying to memorize facts and different laws for each course and create mnemonics that would help me to remember the rules and other legal terminology. Feeling like I didn't belong there to begin with, studying so much, and it still wasn't sticking. It was not easy. I read each of the casebooks more than once, took notes, typed them, and then reread everything over and over. And still, I struggled to master the content and be able to recall all of the information that I needed to for the exams and ultimately the bar exam. I had friends who just "got it" and seemingly did not need to put forth as much effort as I did. They jokingly referred to me as "Overkill Poth" when they saw me surrounded by a pile of law books in the library. Maybe I was overdoing it, but I was not taking any chances with my legal education. I had to do well. I tried not to compare my abilities with theirs, but it was hard at times because I felt myself struggling and felt inferior a lot of the time. Fear of failing kept pushing me to do even more. I wanted to feel confident, but the self-doubt often won.

It was hard to break free from that fear, knowing that so often I had put in the effort and still failed. It happened in law school in my year-long course on property law. I studied all year and for so many hours for the final exam but was unable to answer one essay question. I blanked out. I knew that I would likely fail the test, which would be awful for my GPA. I remember the day I received my grades. I ended up with a C, which is the equivalent of an F in law school. I think I cried for three days. I had given it everything that I could throughout the whole year, and my knowledge came down to two exams. In the end, I knew I couldn't have done better and had to be okay with the grade, but I still felt like a failure. The grade represented *me*, at least in my mind. Knowing that you gave something your all and walking away with a failing grade really stings.

My experiences in law school reminded me how some of my students might be feeling in my classes. For the first time in my teaching career, I understood. I became more in tune with student needs, and better at anticipating misunderstandings. I learned to encourage students more when they expressed doubt about answering, and I was more observant of their non-verbal cues that let me know I needed to try a different strategy and help them through the challenge they might be facing. But I still knew only too well how that pressure and fear of failing could be hard to push aside. Now I am better prepared to share my experience and use it to provide better support for my students.

How can we help students break away from that feeling, especially when we as adults may often feel the same exact thing?

Questions for Reflection

1. When was the last time you took a risk in the classroom? Personally? Did you fail, and did it stop you from trying again?
2. Think about your students. What messages are you sending them by the way you grade, the feedback you give, and the value that is placed on assessments?
3. Has there been a time when you gave up after failing something or before risking a failure? What would you do instead if you had the chance?

SHARE IT OUT!

Share a quote to inspire action to **#FUTURE4EDU**.

Chapter 13

DISRUPTING AND CREATING CHAOS: COMMITTING TO CHANGE FOR THE FUTURE

If you are lucky enough to find a way of life you love, you have to find the courage to live it.

—John Irving

There is comfort in knowing what to expect each day. Having a lesson in mind that has been made with confident, thoughtful planning brings with it some ease, especially for students in our classrooms. But there are times when we cannot follow our plans and need to make changes fast or adapt in the best way that we can.

Schools today are so different. There are issues that we need to be aware of and prepare for in our classrooms and in our professional lives. Issues that most likely did not exist when we were students. The landscape of education is always changing as challenges arise in our schools, new ideas and trends evolve, and we work to find new ways to deal with longstanding issues. Take a moment to think about your why. Consider the actions you take that make others aware of your purpose. Do people know what you stand for? Do you walk with purpose? If your why is only about teaching the content and getting through each year just to repeat the following year, then teaching might seem easy. If this is your why, then you need only to be mindful of and monitor the methods and materials that you use, and keep track of student progress. But if your why is about making a difference in the lives of students, establishing supportive relationships to help them grow, and you are genuinely concerned about them beyond the time they spend with you in the classroom, then you have a much greater responsibility.

With some of the challenges faced in our schools today, such as school violence or helping students to deal with trauma, we need to be fully invested in understanding our students and knowing how to provide for them, no matter what it is that they might need. We can't always prepare for what might happen in the course of a school day, and even the most well-thought-out plans can change. The challenge is finding how we can do all of this during the school day. How can we build in more time to connect with students or take a break in learning when something happens that demands our attention instead? It might mean that we have to cast aside the traditional structure of classrooms and make way for new spaces to foster collaborations and relationships. The structure is not so much about the physical setup of our classrooms. I think it's more about setting up for each of our students. Are we prepared for whatever they may need? Structure is unique to each person.

Unstructured and Better

Structure is an interesting thing. When we think about organizing our spaces and planning our lessons and daily schedules, it's comfortable knowing what to expect, to have a direction to follow, and know our role in it all. For so long, I thought that when it comes to education and the structure of school, everything has to fit in a designated place and time. Rules must be followed, certain teaching methods and standards for communication must be used, and there must be clear expectations when it comes to our professional duties. But teaching is not like it used to be, nor will it stay the same. Changes happen every day, whether because of issues that students are dealing with, new school initiatives, the emergence of new technologies, or other changes that we may not see coming. The only constant is that we have to always be prepared. Fitting all of this into our work can be a challenge. What can we do?

We disrupt the learning experience by creating some chaos in the classroom and finding new and sometimes divergent ways to make changes for good: *good* meaning *better,* and *good* meaning *long-lasting.* And we must be committed to doing so.

Unscripted: Throw Out the Lesson Plan

Do you ever have a lesson prepared, maybe one that you spent a lot of time planning, and for whatever reason you decide at the last minute to stop? For me, there have been times when I've had materials and everything ready to go, until the students arrive. Sometimes I stop because of attendance, due to field trips or absences or students arriving late, and I save the lesson for another day. Other times I change because I notice something in the students: illness, low energy, or another issue that is affecting a large part of the group to the point of distraction. There are times when I immediately sense a complete lack of energy and enthusiasm for learning, which sometimes impacts me and my drive for pushing through. Teachers have their moments too. The excitement I had for the lesson is diminished because I see that the students need my attention more than they need the lesson. Sometimes we need to push aside our plans and our ideas, because we were ready for everything except what showed up in our classrooms on any given day.

How can the child learn to be a free and responsible citizen
when the teacher is bound?

—John Dewey

Amy Storer, Instructional Coach, Keenan Elementary School, Montgomery ISD, @techamys

In 2015, I met a student who would forever change my life. His name is Braeden. One of the first things that he told me was that "we are all robots in this school." That is a pretty powerful statement from a fourth grader. This was the year when all it took was saying yes to change my way of thinking. In my heart, I believed that I was doing all that I could to reach each of my students, but there is always more that can be done! Because when you think about it, growth as an educator should happen naturally if we just step out of our way. I really believe that. We sometimes get so caught up in "that's the way it's always been done" that we forget that our kids deserve more than that. They deserve more from us. It is up to us to equip ourselves with all of the tools and strategies and experiences to reach every single student.

During one of our class assignments, he asked me if he could show his learning by using Minecraft and a screen-casting tool. He was a student who craved so much more than traditional learning. I knew that from day one, so I said yes. That was all it took to not only change my way of thinking but to also strengthen our relationship in the classroom. I was trusting him; therefore, he was trusting me. When he showed me the final product, I had tears in my eyes—tears because he did everything that I had asked him to do, but he did it his own way. He did it in a way that was meaningful to him and connected to something that he enjoyed. I gave him the safe space to use his voice, and I got more from this than I ever would have from the traditional paper and pencil.

I am a better teacher and human being because of my students. College might have awarded me with a degree, but my students, my kids, truly schooled me on school. They were my teachers, well before I even recognized it. They taught me that standing still in this profession is a disservice to them. They taught me that professional growth is just as much for them as it is for me, and that I should want to do better for them. I am a teacher, unbound, because of them, and I am so thankful for that.

●●●

What I love most about Amy's story is that it speaks to the power of relationships, and what a difference those relationships can make in the lives of each of our students and ourselves. While we can have our plans ready, prepped with the best methods and strategies we know of, and although we may be fully invested in making the right decisions for our students, sometimes we have to be willing to step aside because they need something more. Sometimes they just need us, not as a teacher, but as someone who can guide them, give them support, or provide whatever it is they need when they need it. Amy learned from Jed Dearybury, an educator from South Carolina, who said, "Love first, teach second." Everything starts with the heart. We must show our students they matter, that they come first before all else. Amy said something once and it has been a reminder to me each day:

Heart before mind.
Pedagogy before technology.
Process before product.

Planning for the Students

We don't always know what our students might be dealing with when they get to our classrooms—a bad experience or something going on in their lives, or any number of things that we may not see. But their experiences can have a huge impact on the culture of learning for themselves and their classmates. When we notice this, we have two choices: (1) continue with the plan and try to up our game a little to draw the students in, or (2) push whatever we had planned back one more day and instead spend the class period engaging students in a different way. Sometimes it matters more that we connect with each student and wait on the curriculum. Maintaining a positive classroom culture means that we provide the support that students need and are open to making changes that will benefit them in more than just learning the content by providing social-emotional support and showing they come first.

The relationships we have with students will guide us when this happens. When we really know them, we can tell when we need to make a shift in plans because whatever is weighing on them will limit their potential for learning. It's always good to have backup plans in mind for these days, and while it will be something very last minute, we might need to give students a break from the "learning" and take time to recharge. Don't be surprised if students engage more in these types of situations than in the activities that you had planned. Share with students why you are changing the plan. Let them know that you care and recognize when they just need a less structured day to allow for more interactions with peers and with you.

> Nearly every moment of every day, we have the opportunity to give something to someone else—our time, our love, our resources.
>
> —S. Truett Cathy

Support Them Where They Are

Growing up can be tough. Being a teenager brings different stressors, whether academically or socially. We all know the stress of testing and just life as a student in general. There are times when students come in completely wiped out, whether it's because of a high testing time, having a lot of work for classes, or sports or other school events. As a teacher in a small school district, most of my students are involved in multiple activities, so it's not uncommon that they overextend themselves and don't have enough energy left for class. While this can be detrimental to the learning process, if we pushed through with the lesson on those days, how much learning would actually occur? I've tried it and I've seen that for some students it has been a struggle. We end up not getting through the lesson, and there is very little content retained. Other students push through without any issues. But I want to keep all students moving forward, even if they are moving at different paces and with different activities. My thinking has been, *What's the harm in disrupting what I had planned by adding in a little bit of creative chaos to try to lift them up and learn in a more flexible, different, re-energizing way?*

Flexible with Some Limits

I spent many years as a student and I understand the challenges of balancing multiple classes, doing projects, writing essays, and taking tests sometimes on the same day. But I know that part of learning and growing is being able to plan and set a schedule for ourselves. We all need to practice better time management and know the struggle of deadlines. But it comes down to how we choose to spend the time that we have, and I know that students may put off starting a project or studying, leave it to the day it is due, and feel overwhelmed. Even though I know that feeling, I will not change my plan for the day if students ask to have a study hall.

I don't mind providing time for what students call "work days" to catch up on Spanish, practice, or play some games. But I don't give study halls because I've seen "study hall" days turn into "nap time" or "listen to music time" or "play games on the phone time." I guess work days and study hall days might seem like the same thing, but I think "study hall" lessens the accountability. In my mind, study hall implies a place to study or prepare for other classes, or if students tend to nap or listen to music in a regular study hall, they will want to do that in your class too. Work days are not for me to assign busy work and catch up on grading. I expect to be actively moving around the classroom, interacting with individual students or small groups, and helping them to better understand something we covered. Even though times like this diverge from the planned lesson, it is often just what the students and I need.

> In any moment of decision, the best thing you can do is the right thing, the next best thing is the wrong thing, and the worst thing you can do is nothing.
>
> —Theodore Roosevelt

Jon Craig, Instructional Coach, Harry S. Truman High School, Bristol Township School District, @coachjoncraig

We live in a rapidly evolving world, where the newest technologies, standards, research studies, and more are brought before us at a seemingly unprecedented rate. When combined with administrative, political, and community pressures, these tasks can feel impossible. An easy option for teachers can be to shut the classroom door and continue to run the classroom the way it's always been done. However, if we do not look to update our practice, if we do not take risks, if we do not try to use the available data and research to inform our decisions, how can we expect our students to do the same? We must model the learning process we want our students to adopt.

Sometimes we'll do the right thing and we'll cultivate an amazing experience. Unfortunately, at times we'll do the wrong thing and not meet our desired outcomes. In those moments, our students are watching to see how we handle it, which provides us a great opportunity to demonstrate the struggle of a learning process. Both situations can produce desirable results, which have a positive impact on kids. However, we all could agree that no changes and no risks, at best, can produce only the same results, with no growth. Let's bet on our own abilities as educators and take those risks. It won't be the worst thing you could do.

●●●

We've all had moments in our personal and professional lives when we've been afraid to take that first step or scared to try again. In hindsight it might seem so simple, but for some reason it was not so simple at the time. Maybe it was struggling with making a decision, not knowing how to respond to something, or finding our way up when we have been knocked down. It can defeat us if we let it, but we can't because our students and colleagues need us to be at our best. So we dive in and see where the path leads us. As educators, we are often called upon to try new things, to move from our comfort zones and to reflect often. The risks we take can lead us down a greater, more impactful path, not only for us but for those who need us. As Abraham Maslow stated, "In any given moment, we have two options: to step forward into growth or step back into safety."

Holly King, Innovative Educator and Digital Designer, Nags Head, North Carolina, Twitter @hollysking

I sat at my desk, my head spinning with uncertainty. Having just completed an application for a new—and very different—job as a support instructor for gifted students, I questioned whether to click "Submit" on the screen. I had just learned that the future year's schedule moved me back into teaching advanced science courses, my first love and an undeniable passion. After moving to a new district, I had pined for many years for those science courses to open, hence my hesitation about applying for a different position.

Little did I know it, but moving forward in this application process, regardless of the outcome, was a defining fork in my professional career—a fork that forced me to choose between a familiar, comfortable path or a new, uncharted one. As I pondered my decision, my administrator walked in the door and sensed my trepidation. Although our conversation was brief, his words were profound: "You have already taught that course. You know what that is like. Don't you want to try on a different hat and learn new things? Don't you want to grow?"

"Don't you want to grow?" A simple question, isn't it? Yet answering yes was frightening. Answering yes required that I acknowledge that I did not have the answers because I could not see very far down the uncharted path. It meant that I would likely fail in order to grow. It meant that I would need to learn new things with a steep learning curve and build collaborative partnerships with new people. Saying yes meant that I must be vulnerable, risk-tolerant, and growth-minded. Saying yes was uncomfortable and frightening.

Within seconds of his walking out of my door, my decision was made, and I submitted the application. Since that day, those words have been the deciding factor in many decisions, always leading me down a path to tackle a bigger goal or a larger challenge. Single-handedly, this one question, "Don't you want to grow?" has changed my educational trajectory, propelling me to opportunities that I never imagined.

All because I said yes to an opportunity to grow.

•••

It is so important that we not be afraid to take risks, whether in our own classroom with our students or as an administrator with staff. But we also need to challenge ourselves personally and professionally, and that might mean doing something way out of our comfort zones or setting ourselves up for a road of bumps and possibly failures, but ones that will lead us to greater opportunities. We will have to decide, and then go and grow from that decision.

Questions for Reflection

1. Take one day where you have a lesson plan prepared, and at some point during the class make a shift and ask students for ideas on how to continue. How did it feel to make that change, and how did the students respond? Feel free to share to #FUTURE4EDU.

2. Being present and greeting our students and our colleagues is important for building school culture; however, having enough time can be a challenge. What are some ways to build in time to the day to make sure these interactions happen?

3. Think about times where class was interrupted, technology failed, or due to some other cause you could not get through your planned lesson. We need to be flexible in our instruction and be prepared for the unexpected. Brainstorm a few ideas to work around these bumps in the lesson plan. Share your ideas in backup plans to #FUTURE4EDU.

SHARE IT OUT!

Share an idea for an "on the fly" activity to cause some creative chaos in your classroom. Share it to **#FUTURE4EDU.**

Final Thoughts

WHERE DO WE GO FROM HERE?

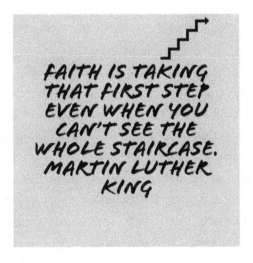

FAITH IS TAKING
THAT FIRST STEP
EVEN WHEN YOU
CAN'T SEE THE
WHOLE STAIRCASE.
MARTIN LUTHER
KING

As the famous human rights activist Malcolm X once said, "Education is the passport to the future, for tomorrow belongs to those who prepare for it today." Preparing for the uncertainties of the future will require us to foster a supportive environment for learning and a network where all "learners" (educators and students) connect and empower one another. We are better together. We must unite in the role of "learner" and model curiosity for learning by becoming co-learners with students rather than "sages on the stage."

Remember: It's Not About Us

As I took a walk one day in April, I thought about how education has changed over the past twenty-five years since I student-taught and began my teaching career. How have I changed, and how has the role of an educator changed? When we all start teaching, before meeting our students for the first time, I think that initially, everything was about *us*. Asking ourselves: How do we prepare for class? Would we be able to handle situations that come up in class without losing our confidence? Would we know all of the policies, the content that we're responsible for teaching, the best methods to use to meet our students' needs? All of this was about us.

And what I realized while walking and recording my thoughts, is that when we meet our students for the first time, whether on the first day we teach at a new school or the first job that we have out of school, is when we make that shift from it being about *us* to being about *them*. Our focus and our motivation shift to being about the students.

The reason we get up in the morning, it's not for that hot cup of coffee or warm breakfast, which are nice, but the reason we get up every morning is for our students. We do what it takes to bring our best selves every day because they deserve nothing less.

Future-Ready

In their book *Empower*, A. J. Juliani and John Spencer state, "Our job is not to prepare students for something, our job is to prepare students for anything." As educators, we must ask ourselves, "What are the skills that students should develop regardless of what the future holds in terms of education?" While we cannot predict exactly what the jobs of the future will be, we know the world will continue to undergo many changes. We can base our predictions only on staying informed of trends and skills that are applicable to life and work. Skills like leadership, collaboration, communication, and time management will be necessary, and as educators we can best prepare students by offering diverse ways for students to interact with the content and one another. We must be prepared to do more than just teach the content, and instead actively seek ways to connect students with learning that extends beyond the classroom space to global learning opportunities.

Facing the Uncertainty of the Future

Over the past year I've been researching topics such as the future of work, the future of learning and the implications of technologies like Artificial Intelligence for education and jobs of the future. It's amazing how the world has changed in terms of how, when, and where students can learn, how easily we connect globally, and especially the increase in the tools and technologies available which make learning and connecting easier than ever before. We need to know how we can best prepare our students for jobs which we can't be sure will still exist in the future. Another challenge is that we cannot predict the types of jobs that might exist five, ten or fifteen years in the future, when our youngest students in kindergarten will be making the decision to pursue further education or to enter the workforce. We must decide, with everything that we know now, what is it that we provide in our schools that will not become outdated in the next couple of years? What knowledge and skills will be applicable to whatever it is our students might encounter in their future? How can we best prepare students for a future which is yet unknown?

We know that today's students need a variety of skills, the often-referred-to

"21st century skills." We must determine the best ways to provide authentic, unique, and innovative learning experiences to prepare students for jobs which may not exist yet in our ever-changing world.

Move beyond the traditional curriculum and teaching methods, and instead provide ways for students to more actively learn and explore the world. In doing so, hopefully and ideally, no matter what students ultimately decide to do and whatever the future holds, they will have skills, real-world awareness, and flexibility, and be well-equipped for a constantly changing system.

Schools around the country have started to offer more courses based on emerging trends and making "predictions" for future-ready skills. Some courses or components of courses available in schools, including my own, are entrepreneurship, web design, sports and entertainment management, and STEM curriculum, which teach content and provide opportunities for students to design their own learning journeys. As educators we sometimes assume that students already have certain skills, such as knowing how to use and leverage technology effectively, because they have grown up in a technology-infused world. However, the reality for many students is quite different. We need to make sure that students have time to learn basic skills, and then can push themselves to go beyond.

How Can Students Learn Best?

In a speech about the future of learning, Alan November, international keynote speaker and author, said we have to "teach students how to learn."[1] Students know how to find one answer; they have grown accustomed to more objective assessments and applications of learning, rather than subjective, where they have room to explore and determine how to show their learning. We need to move beyond tasks and experiences that have one right answer,

---

1   Getting Smart. (2019). 21st-Century Skills We Need to Cultivate in Students | Getting Smart. [online] Available at: https://www.gettingsmart.com/2018/03/21st-century-skills-we-need-to-cultivate-in-students.

and instead engage students in learning that goes beyond the basic recall of content and instead helps students to develop persistence and resilience by engaging in productive struggle and deeper levels of thinking.

An article that I came across during my research included five essential Montessori conditions for creating an innovative workplace.[2] The conditions were:

- Dedicating time for creative projects
- Rewarding innovation and divergent ideas
- Empowering employees to make decisions
- Allowing for failure
- Measuring what matters most

After giving it some thought, I realized that these are the exact conditions that we should aim to foster for our students. Within our school community and by connecting with our PLN, together we can provide more innovative learning opportunities for all students and not just those in our own classrooms. Students need to have independence in designing their learning path, opportunities to pursue their interests and connect with the real world, and more importantly, to be challenged in the work that they do. There are several ways that we can provide these opportunities for our students today:

- Project-based learning (PBL) will promote student choice and engage students in sustained inquiry. PBL promotes critical thinking, creativity, problem-solving, and enhances the learning potential for each student through real-world learning experiences that connect them in a more meaningful way within their community and globally.

---

2   Getting Smart. (2019). Enhancing Innovation in the Workplace through Five Montessori Conditions. [online] Available at: https://www.gettingsmart.com/2019/03/enhancing-innovation-in-the-workplace-through-five-montessori-conditions/.

• Place-based learning is a way to use specific locations and shift from the traditional content for a course, to instead use the geography, or even culture of a place, to help master the content knowledge while also developing empathy and social-emotional learning skills. With place-based learning, we connect students with real-world experiences that enable them to apply the content in an authentic and more meaningful way. It gives students the chance to explore the world more and become personally invested in their work. These learning opportunities also promote the development of social-emotional learning (SEL) skills, which are vital for students' personal and professional growth.

• The use and implementation of emerging technologies such as artificial intelligence and augmented and virtual reality will likely continue to increase in the future. With estimates of 40 percent of the jobs of the future being replaced by artificial intelligence, and the increase in the use of AR and VR for fields including healthcare, the business sector, education, and the military, to name a few, students need time to investigate these areas. Educators need to know how to use these technologies to engage students in learning and encourage students to explore more and become the designers of the tools we need for the future.

• Building the entrepreneurial skills of our students is another way to help students prepare for a changing work landscape. With the uncertainty surrounding the types of jobs that will exist in the future, students need to be able to quickly adapt to a changing work landscape. Through courses or experiences that promote independent as well as collaborative learning, critical thinking, problem-solving, and promote the development of social-emotional learning (SEL) skills, we can give all students a more solid foundation of skills that will be applicable to whatever they do in the future. We need to help students think like entrepreneurs and become the innovators of the future.

- Preparing students for a future of careers in STEM, and with computer science and coding skills. In 2015, there were seven million openings in jobs in areas such as art and design that rely on coding skills. Current estimates are that 58 percent of the new jobs available in STEM are in computing; however, only 10 percent of STEM graduates are in the field of computer science.[3] Looking to future employment for students, computing jobs are the number one source of new wages in the United States, and this is a number that is expected to increase at twice the rate of other jobs.

These are just some ideas for educators to pursue. One thing that I recommend is thinking beyond the content area or grade level that you teach, and instead focus on how you can involve students in these types of learning experiences. Regardless of whether you teach kindergarten, middle school students, or high school seniors, we are all responsible for preparing our students for our future. For a long time I thought that I had to follow traditional teaching methods and materials, but I was wrong. And I was wrong because I didn't look for new ideas because I kept myself in isolation. Start today, if you haven't already, by reaching out to colleagues, your PLN, and most definitely to your students. Challenge yourselves to explore one of these areas together, co-design, collaborate, and take some risks together.

Learning Should Be Different

As educators, we must stay informed about what the future of education and work look like, what skills our students need, and the best ways we can

---

3   Code.org. (2019). Blurbs and Stats. [online] Available at: https://hourofcode.com/us/ promote/stats.

work together to help them develop those skills. Regardless of our specific roles in education, we all have the same responsibility to students. It is important that we connect with our students, let them know where they are on their learning path, how they got there, and where they can go next. John Hattie found that 95 percent of what teachers do to enhance student achievement works, which is why building the relationships and showing that we genuinely care about their well-being and success are vital to their growth.[4] Hattie identified six important qualities of teachers that greatly impact student learning. In summary, they are passionate about helping students learn, observant and cognizant of their impact on students, clear about what students are learning, build strong relationships, implement evidence-based strategies, and engage in ongoing professional growth. With our support and intentional investment in our students, they will become leaders, designers, problem solvers and innovators.

The future of the world is in our classrooms today.
—Ivan Welton Fitzwater

Ask the Students

In learning and growing as educators, we can learn just as much, if not more, from our students as they do from us. What helps us to improve in our profession can come from many sources, but the feedback we get from our students is truly going to enable us to provide the best learning experiences for them. Take a risk and ask your students to become the co-designers in the classroom; show them that they are valued and that their voices matter.

Two of my students, Cassy and Celaine, have presented with me at conferences, written blog posts, contributed a chapter to a book, and have been advocates for, and passionate about, student-driven learning and the power of

---

4   Fastiggi, W., and Hattie, J. (2010). *Visible learning: A synthesis of over 800 meta-analyses relating to achievement.* London: Routledge.

choice. As seniors who are ready to step into the next phase of their learning journey, they offer their advice to teachers everywhere:

> We urge teachers to continue to have faith and confidence in their students. We believe in the power of learning and in having an education, and the difference it can make in a student's life. It is so important to teach students in a way that inspires them to take action and go forward to do great things.

So here are our thoughts, as current students, to any teacher:

Be creative.
Take risks to enhance learning.
Be supportive.
Make connections.
Create opportunities.
Encourage and inspire.
Be the inspiration so students know they matter.

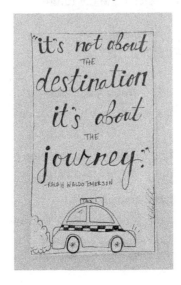

We all need to take the time to look at ourselves closely. Who are we and who do we want to be? Who do we need to be? What is our why? What is the one thing that you are so passionate about that you are willing to take risks, to accept defeat, and to invest yourself completely without wanting anything in return, other than to know that you've done the best that you could, with what you had at that time?

What experiences have defined you? Whether positive or negative, what memories do you have of your own teachers and of the way you learned best? Where did you start from, and where are you now on your journey of life and of growing as an educator? What is your spark?

> Change almost never fails because it's too early. It almost
> always fails because it's too late.
> —Seth Godin

Start today. How can you prepare for the future? Share who you are, your strengths and weaknesses. In your weakness, someone else will find strength. Failure is a necessary part of learning. In the book *Drive*, Daniel Pink wrote, "Start small and pile up small wins." As educators, we know that we still learn from failures. Instead of focusing on what we have not accomplished *yet*, we need to ask ourselves, via Daniel Pink: "Was I a little better today than yesterday?"[5] Think about the progress that you make each day, and use your experiences to help students face their own challenges. Share your story, because we fail and learn better when we connect. You don't need to walk alone in isolation anymore. Welcome to the future.

QUESTIONS FOR REFLECTION

1. What would happen if you decided not to follow your lesson plan for one class period? How could you quickly come up with a new plan?
2. Think of a time when you had to make a decision or take action in a moment you didn't plan. Was it right or was it wrong? Whether it was right or wrong, how was it better than inaction?
3. What flags or indicators can you make for yourself to prevent

---

5 Pink, Daniel H. *Drive: The Surprising Truth About What Motivates Us.* New York: Riverhead Books,U.S., 2013. pages 156 and 176.

inaction in the future and limit your fears of making the wrong decision? How can you inspire others to do the same?

SHARE IT OUT!

What is one of your favorite last-minute backup plans that always works? Share to **#FUTURE4EDU.**

Additional Suggested Reading:

Culturize, Jimmy Casas

Daring Greatly, Brené Brown

Divergent EDU, Mandy Froehlich

Drive, Daniel Pink

Empower, A.J. Juliani and John Spencer

Four O'Clock Faculty, Rich Czyz

Innovator's Mindset, George Couros

Lead Like A Pirate, Beth Houf and Shelley Burgess

Let Them Speak, Rebecca Coda and Rick Jetter

Social LEADia, Jennifer Casa-Todd

The Path to Serendipity, Allyson Apsey

Teach Like a Pirate, Dave Burgess

The Fire Within, Mandy Froehlich

Take the L.E.A.P.: Ignite a Culture of Innovation, Elisabeth Bostwick

Visible Learning, John Hattie

What School Could Be, Ted Dintersmith

A Passion for Kindness, Tamara Letter

The Revolution: It's Time to Empower Change in Our Schools,
Darren Ellwein and Derek L. McCoy

Start With Why, Simon Sinek

In Other Words, Rachelle Dene Poth

Make Learning Magical, Tisha Richmond

ABOUT THE AUTHOR

Rachelle Dene Poth is a longtime French, Spanish and STEAM teacher and an EdTech Consultant, and the founder of THRIVEinEDU, LLC. She is also an attorney and has a master's degree in Instructional Technology. Rachelle serves as president of the ISTE Teacher Education Network and communications chair for the Mobile Learning Network. She received the Presidential Gold Award for Volunteer Service to Education in 2018, Silver Award in 2017, and was selected as one of "20 to watch" by the NSBA and the PAECT Outstanding Teacher of the Year in 2017. Rachelle is a Future Ready Instructional Coach. She is an Edugladiator Core Warrior and an affiliate of the Pushing Boundaries Consulting, LLC. Rachelle received the gold award in 2018 and 2019, and the ISTE Making IT Happen Award in 2019.

Rachelle is the author of *In Other Words: Quotes That Push Our Thinking*, and is working on two other books which are due in 2019. She is a contributing author to several books, including *EduMatch Snapshot in Education 2016, 2017, 2018*, and *Gamify Literacy*, an ISTE publication. She also wrote a chapter in the book *Stories in EDU*. She is a blogger for DefinedSTEM and Getting Smart. She is the host of #Formativechat on Mondays, and maintains her "Learning as I Go" blog site at www.Rdene915.com. Connect with Rachelle on Twitter @Rdene915.

CPSIA information can be obtained
at www.ICGtesting.com
Printed in the USA
BVHW030017040919
557511BV00001B/4/P